FACTS
VERSUS
FICTION

The True Story of the Jonathan Years, Chibok, 2015 and the Conspiracies

RENO OMOKRI

TABLE OF CONTENTS

DEDICATION

This book is dedicated to my father and mother, Peter and Mercy, who have been married 55 years this year (2017) and to my dear friend, the late, great Oronto Natei Douglas, who introduced me to Dr. Goodluck Jonathan who has now become my friend and big brother. Finally, this book is also dedicated to Emmanuel Bamidele Orevba, who died of a heart attack on April 23, 2011 as he celebrated the victory of Dr. Goodluck Jonathan in the 2011 Nigerian presidential election.

FOREWORD

Seeking to find the truth in Nigeria is like looking into a constantly changing kaleidescope -as soon as you think you have discerned a picture it shifts again.

However if you want a clear view of what went on behind the scenes during the administration ofGoodluck Jonathan you would be well served by reading this new book by Reno Omokri who served as one his three spokesmen and who is now a Pastor in California as well as the Founder of an orphanage in Benin, the launch of which I had the privilege of attending.

The key case he makes that there was a conspiracy to evict Goodluck from the Presidency with the active collusion of Obama and the American Government is very compelling and is made compelling by his technique of posing simple questions set in the context ofevents that are in the public domain which thus allows the reader to make up their own mind.

For example, why did the US State Department prevent the sale of military hardware to help the Nigerian army tackle Boko Haram on the grounds ofhuman rights yet sell them to its neighbours who have a significantly worse record?

The timing of the book is rather topical given the current furor about the involvement ofRussia in the recent US election, which makes an interesting counter-point to read about America's sticky hands in Nigeria's affairs. Surely something the Land of the Free has never been complicit in before?

The complexity of Nigerian politics has not changed over the years from the zoning policy determining whose turn it is between the Muslim north or the Christian south to rule the country, to the legacy of corruption which has flowed from the curse ofblack gold and stultified economic development of this resource and people-rich country.

Nigeria is a country I have been to 48 times and for which I have a huge admiration, despite its many undoubted challenges and frustrations. It is the only country I know where the advertising in a newspaper is more trusted than its editorial, so sorting 'Fact from Fiction' is a significant challenge - especially when the response ofpeople on the other side of an argument is to shout louder and attack their opponents with a vitriol that is as pugnacious as it is loquacious. The enlightening aspect of this book is its quiet reasoning and whilst the author does of course 'stand where he sits' the book does provide a more considered perspective from the Goodluck camp of a critical crossroads in the nation's history than anything else that has been published to-date.

Michael Moszynski,
Founder and CEO of LONDON Advertising

INTRODUCTION

I decided to write this book for the simple reason that it will be irresponsible for people like me, who had a front toe seat in the in the arena ofleadership in Nigeria between 2011 and 2015 to sit idly by and watch as history is distorted and revised to suit predetermined ends.

Coming from a family with a long history ofjurisprudence, my father taught me more than once that no matter how far falsehood has traveled, it must eventually be overtaken by truth.

This work therefore is just an attempt to do my part in laying bare the fact and shine the light on the truth. My work is not very hard in this regard because as Augustine ofHippo said "The truth is like a lion; you don't have to defend it. Let it loose; it will defend itself." In this work you will find dates, names, places and exact figures. This is deliberate. Such specificity is to make it easy for anyone who doubts the veracity of these facts to come up with their own truths. It is commonly said that people are entitled to their opinions but not to the facts.

I find it most uncharitable that a man who verifiably has done more than most to extend democracy in Africa and Nigeria should be repaid back by pseudo democrats in coins that he does not deserve.

The theory ofproofby assertions is such that a lie told so many times will eventually be passed offas the truth if it is not challenged and ifall others have been intimidated to such an extent as to be unwilling to tell the truth, I will never be amongst those. Those who raised me, raised me up to believe that there is nobody important enough to lie to or be intimidated by on earth.

Doctor Goodluck Jonathan took Nigeria to greater heights and transformed her from a low-income nation to a middle-income nation that became and still is the largest economy in the continent ofAfrica and the third fastest growing economy in the world. Under his leadership, Nigeria made the most advancement in life expectancy and human happiness according to indexes from the United Nations.

And he did this while facing some of the most vicious forms of terrorism known to man in the form of the Boko Haram insurgency, and perhaps the most virulent pandemic the world could ever face in the form of the Ebola Virus. How did he and his team do it? How was he able to stay focused enough to achieve such great feats amid an orchestrated distraction by those who promised to make "Nigeria ungovernable for him".

This book will answer these and many other such questions and long after the purveyors ofuntruths are gone from the political space of Nigeria, history will record the years between 2010 and 2015 as Nigeria's Golden Years that brought about unprecedented transformation from a man who saw himselfas a pencil in God's hands and vowed that 'my political ambition is not worth the blood of any Nigerian'!

Reno Omokri
May, 2017.

Chapter 1
THE CONSPIRACY TO REMOVE JONATHAN

The recent revelations from Segun Adeniyi's book, *Against the Run of Play: How an Incumbent President was Defeated in Nigeria*, have promoted reactions and counter Treactions to some of the more astounding accounts detailed in that book.

Former President Jonathan in his interview with Segun Adeniyi, gave some detail of a conspiracy to remove him from office due to patriotic policies and actions he undertook which might have set him at variance with foreign powers.

Amongst other things, Adeniyi quotes Dr. Goodluck Jonathan as saying "I got on very well with Prime Minister David Cameron but at some point, I noticed that the Americans were putting pressure on him and he had to join them against me. But I didn't know how far President Obama was prepared to go to remove me until France caved into the pressure from America."

Since these revelations came to light, a former Governor of Niger state, Mr. Babangida Aliyu has also been quoted making comments in Segun Adeniyi's book that corroborate the statements by Dr. Jonathan.

According to Mr. Aliyu, the Obama administration had invited twelve governors from Northern Nigeria to sound them out on their commitment to the plot to unseat Dr. Jonathan.

Mr. Aliyu is quoted in Segun Adeniyi's book as saying "I have no proo-fofcourse, but I think the idea was to ascertain what the disposition of the north would be to the idea ofanother term for President Jonathan. That was my reading of the situation. I believe it was all about the 2015 election for which the Americans had resolved not to support Jonathan. They just wanted to size us up for the level ofcommitment to regime change."

Mr. Aliyu was referring to a series ofmeetings that twelve Northern governors had in the U.S. in March 2014.

Why did the Obama administration organize those meetings? What occurred at those meetings? Who said what, where, when and why? The answer to those questions will help throw light on if there was a conspiracy by the Obama administration (not the United States) to remove then President Jonathan from office.

I tracked down Mr. Matthew T. Page who until his resignation in 2016 was the U.S. State Department's top intelligence analyst on Nigeria. Matthew Page also served as Deputy National Intelligence Officer for Africa with the National Intelligence Council. He sat in on each of the meetings the twelve Northern Nigerian governors attended, beginning from their meetings at the United States Institute for Peace and thereafter their meetings at the State Department.

In 2016, Mr. Page left the State Department and moved to Cambridge in the United Kingdom from where he spoke to me. He was adamant that Mr. Babangida Aliyu's version of the events at those meetings where not accurate and was keen to set the records straight.

According to Mr. Page, the meetings were attended by twelve Northern governors of whom the most vocal was the then governor of Adamawa state, Admiral Murtala Nyako. Others at the meetings who voiced anti Jonathan sentiments were then Kano governor, Rabiu Musa Kwankwaso, Aliyu Wammako of Sokoto and Kashim Shettima of Borno. The then governors of Kwara and Kogi were in attendance but were non-committal.

Mr. Page noted that the meetings at the United States Institute for Peace were innocuous but that when the governors proceeded to the closed-door sessions at the US State Department, things changed.

According to Mr. Page, present at the State Department meetings were Ambassador Linda Thomas Greenfield who was then the Assistant Secretary of State for African Affairs in the Department of State's Bureau of African Affairs. Also present at the meeting was the then number three man at the State Department, Ambassador Thomas Alfred "Tom" Shannon Jr., acting Deputy Secretary of State of the United States and the Under Secretary of State for Political Affairs.

At that meeting, Admiral Murtala Nyako read out a memo he had written itemizing the case against Jonathan. He was so openly and almost violently against the Jonathan administration in his speech that he had to be openly rebuked at the meeting by the then Nigerian ambassador to the US, Ambassador Adebowale Adefuye of blessed memory.

Admiral Nyako's belligerence against the Jonathan administration was so venomous that it prompted a rebuttal from the Gombe state governor, Ibrahim Hassan Dankwambo, who showed loyalty to the then Nigerian President. According to Mr. Page, this prompted most of the other Northern governors present to turn on him.

In my interview with him, Mr. Page revealed to me that after the anti Jonathan tirades by these governors, they were shepherded to the White House on March 18, 2014 for more meetings. Even though Mr. Page attended the reception at the White House for the Northern governors, he did not make me privy to who were at that particular meeting other than stating that the governors met with then National Security Adviser, Susan Rice. Ms. Rice is however a known Nigerian specialist and was the person who on July 7, 1998, made the tea that the presumed winner of the June 12, 1993 Nigerian Presidential election, chief MKO Abiola, drank minutes before passing away after reportedly foaming at the mouth.

After the meeting, the Obama White House released a statement which said, amongst other things;

"Rice and the governors discussed the need to bring an end to the violence and insurgency in northern Nigeria; create broad-based economic opportunity in the north and throughout Nigeria; protect and respect human rights; strengthen democratic governance; and ensure that the 2015 election in Nigeria are free and fair."

What the White House statement did not say, but which I verified from other sources, was that at that meeting, Admiral Nyako accused then President Jonathan of being behind Boko Haram, the Islamic terrorist group that is behind the insurgency in Nigeria's Northeast (the same accusation was publicly made by Nasir El-rufai in 2014. El-rufai was one of a handle of All Progressive Congress party officials that related directly with David Axelrod's firm as AKPD Message and Media prepared the APC for the 2015 elections).

One question arises though, when sub national officials from a nation that is friendly to the United States espouse comments that undermine the President of that friendly nation, why would such persons be honored with very high level meetings that stretched from the State Department to the White House?

When I asked Mr. Page if he thought that the Obama administration was opposed to the re-election of the then Nigerian President, Goodluck Jonathan, he paused and said "my objective opinion is that it was not as if the administration was against Jonathan. There were a few issues. The Obama administration was a bit disappointed (I know that sounds paternalistic) but there were some issues they felt let down on, and you have to remember that the Obama administration supported the transfer of power to Jonathan in 2010. The issues were the human rights situation in the Northeast which has still not changed under Buhari and Diezani Alison-Madueke who they felt should have been removed. There were some issues with some clauses in the Same Sex Marriage (Prohibition) Bill 2013".

Mr. Page continuing said "there were some at the embassy in Nigeria who were actually anti Buhari because of his failure to call his followers to order and stop the post-election violence of 2011".

Although he listed three reasons why the Obama administration felt let down on by Dr. Jonathan, my conversation with Mr. Page gave me a sense that the first two reasons were just excuses and that the main reason was because of the Same Sex Marriage (Prohibition) Bill 2013.

That issue was a deal breaker for the Obama administration because of the strong support they had from the LGBT (Lesbian, Gay, Bisexual or Transgender) community for Mr Obama's re-election campaign of 2012.

Per the New York Times, the gay vote was "crucial" to Obama's re-election, whereas to CNN, the LGBT community not only made the difference in 2012 by trooping out to vote for Obama, they were also his top donors.

In Tracy Baim's book, Obama and the Gays: A Political Marriage, she details the influence that the former American President wields with the LGBT community. Very few voting blocs have the get out the vote power that the LGBT community has, being that they are great at organizing for the purpose of advancing their agenda.

I had a firsthand experience of this on April 23, 2016 when I represented Dr. Goodluck Jonathan at a keynote lecture at the California State University in Sacramento. The LGBT community found out that Dr. Jonathan was to speak at the university and organized a protest and a rally against the event which was big enough to attract news coverage from Fox News and when I arrived the event I had to meet with leaders of the LGBT community to persuade them that the Same Sex Marriage (Prohibition) Bill 2013 did not originate from Dr. Jonathan as they erroneously believed, although he signed it as was constitutionally required of him.

There are those that believe that in exchange for their strong support for Obama, they extracted some concessions from him, one of which being to use the full force of his executive powers to advance the course of the LGBT community worldwide, including undermining any foreign government that was perceived to be against same sex marriages and or domestic partnerships.

In fact, after a July 25, 2013 reception at Number 10 Downing Street, held to celebrate the legalization of gay marriage in the United Kingdom, Obama ally and then U.K. Prime Minister, David Cameron, boasted that he was committed to exporting gay marriage around the world. His exact words were, "I am going to export the Bill."

Five months after Cameron made that pledge, Dr. Jonathan, as Nigerian President, signed the Same Sex Marriage (Prohibition) Bill 2013 on January 13, 2014 putting him in direct opposition to both President Obama and Prime Minister Cameron.

Recall that Dr. Jonathan had said "I got on very well with Prime Minister David Cameron but at some point, I noticed that the Americans were putting pressure on him and he had to join them against me."

When I asked him when he felt a change in his relationship with Cameron, former President Jonathan said "sometime in early 2014". Could it be a coincidence that early 2014 is also the same time he signed the law criminalizing same sex marriage in Nigeria?

But back to the 2014 meetings, the interesting thing about these meetings is that the Obama administration did not try to balance them out by having other high-level meetings of similar status for governors from Southern Nigeria. Now why would they act this way knowing that Nigeria as a nation was created by amalgamating the two separate nations of Southern Nigeria and Northern Nigeria by the British government in 1914.

Another interesting connection is that these high-level meetings arranged for Northern governors by the Obama administration took place in 2014, at the same time Obama's confidante and former White House Senior Advisor, David Axelrod's firm, AKPD Message and Media, began to work as a paid consultant for the then Nigerian opposition party, All Progressive Congress, which was the vehicle through which incumbent President Muhammadu Buhari rose to power.

Coincidence? You tell me.

Let us connect some more dots.

One of the governors who was most vociferous against Dr. Jonathan at those meetings was Governor Kashim Shettima of Borno state. Bear in mind that he and his colleagues had a closed-door meeting with the then US National Security Adviser, Ms. Susan Rice, on March 18, 2014. Is it a coincidence then that three weeks after Governor Shettima returned from his meeting with Ms. Rice, Boko Haram struck at Chibok town and kidnapped two hundred and seventy six girls at Government Secondary School Chibok?

The meeting with Ms. Rice occurred on March 18, 2014, the kidnap of the Chibok girls occurred on April 14, 2014. Prudent minded persons may be wise to take a second look at the Chibok kidnapping.

For starters, for the first three weeks after the kidnapping, the story did not gain traction in the international media, but something unusual happened on May 10, 2014. Every week, President Barack Obama gave a Presidential Address to the US public. On May 10, 2014, for the first time ever, President Obama asked his wife, First Lady Michelle Obama, to deliver the weekly Presidential Address in his stead. The previous week, she had tweeted a picture where she held up a sign that had the hashtag, #BringBackOurGirls.

Speaking to the American public, Mrs. Obama said:

"What happened in Nigeria was not an isolated incident. It's a story we see every day as girls around the world risk their lives to pursue their ambitions.

"I want you to know that Barack has directed our government to do everything possible to support the Nigerian government's efforts to find these girls and bring them home. In these girls, Barack and I see our own daughters. We see their hopes, their dreams, and we can only imagine the anguish their parents are feeling right now."

The #BringBackOurGirls hashtag went ballistic and instantly became a cause celebre with music super stars and international celebrities imitating Mrs. Obama's gesture. Why is this piece of information important? Remember that a senior member of the APC boasted publicly that the #BringBackOurGirls movement was 'founded by our members' . In the next chapter, I dwell on this issue in more detail, but there are still more dots to connect.

The US meetings of Northern governors was arranged by the United States Institute for Peace, with the support of the U.S. State Department's Bureau of Conflict and Stabilization Operations. One of the purposes of the meeting was to discuss "strategies for stabilization and development in northern Nigeria.

Now note that word 'stabilization'. The purpose of that meeting was to hold discussions with Northern governors on how to bring stability to Northern Nigeria amongst other things.

On more than one occasion, President Muhammadu Buhari has publicly thanked the Obama administration for its help in the elections that brought him to power. Now note the choice of words that President Buhari used on one of such occasions.

On the 20th of July 2015, President Muhammadu Buhari was received by then US President, Barack Obama at the White House. During that meeting, Buhari said:

"Nigeria will be ever grateful to President Obama and the United States for making Nigeria consolidate its gains on democracy."

President Buhari also said that 'the unrelenting pressure on the immediate past administration by the United States and some European countries made the general elections in Nigeria to be free and fair.'

Fast forward to the 12th of July, 2016 and President Buhari was playing host to Obama's outgoing ambassador to Nigeria, James F Entwistle, at the Aso Rock Presidential villa.

At that meeting, President Buhari said:

"The U.S. support before, during and after the 2015 elections was vital to Nigeria's stability and I will never forget the role they played in the stability of Nigeria."

Note the use of that word 'stability'.

Notable figures within the US diplomatic circles have for long held the view that Northern Nigeria's absence from the front seat of political power in Nigeria fueled the discontentment that expressed itself in different types of agitations that affect the stability of Nigeria.

Indeed, some have cited the 2010 comments by a notable Northern elder to buttress this view.

On October 10, 2010, a Northern elder, Alhaji Lawal Kaita, from the same state (Katsina) as President Muhammadu Buhari said:

"The North is determined, if that happens (Jonathan contesting and winning the 2011 election), to make the country ungovernable for President Jonathan or any other Southerner who finds his way to the seat of power on the platform of the PDP against the principle of the party's zoning policy".

When you consider this statement and the meetings that were held with

Northern governors leading up to the run up of the 2015 elections by the Obama administration, you begin to understand why that word 'stability' is more than just a word.

Also recall that the Obama administration refused to sell weapons to Nigeria and cited the Leahy Law as a hindrance because the law prevents the US from selling weapons to nations whose armies have violated human rights.

When Nigeria tried to buy weapons from other nations (most notably Israel), the Obama administration blocked the sale making Nigeria so desperate for weapons that she had to go to the Black Market.

Ironically, just as the Obama administration was refusing to provide support to Nigeria's military in their anti-terror war, the same administration provided major military aid to Chad, Niger and Mali to help their anti-terror war.

But according to Amnesty International, all three of these nations (Chad, Niger and Mali) have as bad and in some cases even a worse human rights record than Nigeria.

So why were they considered deserving of military aid and support by the Obama administration and Nigeria under Jonathan was not.

Thank God the Trump administration has signified its intention to sell weapons to Nigeria. Indeed, the Trump administration has revealed plans to sell 12 Embraer A-29 Super Tucano aircraft with sophisticated targeting gear for nearly $600 million to Nigeria.

What has changed? The human rights situation in Nigeria has not improved. According to an inquiry by the Kaduna state government of Nigeria, in December of 2015 the Nigerian Army slaughtered 347 Shia Muslims many of whom were women and children. There were allegedly state sponsored protests against Amnesty International in March of 2017 because of the organization's report citing that gross human right violations are still occurring in the Northeast.

So rather than the human rights situation improving, it has become worse! The Leahy Law has not changed. It remains on the US statute books.

The ability of the Trump administration to sell weapons to Nigeria despite the Leahy Law proves that the law was used as an excuse to deprive the Jonathan administration of urgently needed weapons to frustrate its anti-terror war and thus affect its popularity.

If you think this is far fetched, then consider that, according to the Los Angeles Times, this current sale of weapons to Nigeria by the Trump administration was actually initiated by the Obama administration at the tail end of that government.

Despite the refusal of the Obama administration to sell weapons to Nigeria for the prosecution of Nigeria's anti-terror war against Boko Haram insurgents, Obama sent his Secretary of State, John Kerry, to Nigeria on January 25, 2015, to pressure the Jonathan administration not to postpone the Presidential elections even though he was aware that going ahead with the election on February 14, 2015, at a time when Boko Haram controlled huge swathes of territory, would mean disenfranchising those Nigerians in the Local Government Areas that Boko Haram held in Borno state at that time.

Professor Attahiru Jega, the chairman of the Independent Electoral Commission had said while announcing the postponement of the election that "calling people to exercise their democratic rights in a situation where their security cannot be guaranteed is a most onerous responsibility".

To this, Mr. Kerry responded by saying "political interference with the Independent National Electoral Commission is unacceptable and it is critical that the government not use security concerns as a pretext for impeding the democratic process."

How postponing an election, within the time frame allowed by Nigerian law, would mean "impeding the democratic process", when the postponement was done purposely to flush out Boko Haram and allow people who would not have been able to vote had the postponement not taken place was never explained by Mr. Kerry.

Finally, consider the subliminal messages that were communicated by President Obama when he took the unusual step of addressing Nigerians on March 23, 2015 just five days to the presidential elections on March 28, 2019.

On that broadcast, Obama told Nigerians:

"Now you have an historic opportunity to help write the next chapter of Nigeria's progress by voting in the upcoming elections.....Boko Haram wants to destroy Nigeria and all that you have built. By casting your ballot, you can help secure your nation's progress."

Note the words 'next chapter'. During the present fourth republic, Nigeria had four successful presidential elections before 2015. 2014 was not a 'next chapter'. The only way it would have been a next chapter would be for the incumbent to be unseated by the opposition. And that, in my opinion, was the subliminal message President Obama was passing across.

Secondly, note the sentence "By casting your ballot you can help secure your nation's progress." When you consider that according to the Los Angeles Times, it was only after the election of Muhammadu Buhari that the Obama administration approved the sale of weapons to Nigeria (which the Trump administration is now implementing), those words by Obama take on a new meaning.

Could it be that he was passing on a subliminal message to the Nigerian people that if they were tired of being slaughtered by Boko Haram they were to vote for the right candidate and, voila, the Leahy Law would no longer be a hindrance to the purchase of weapons by Nigeria?

Obama's words appear to have deeper intent when you connect them to the words of his Vice President, Joe Biden.

After President Buhari's victory at the polls, then US Vice President, Joe Biden called him to congratulate him. According to the White House transcript of the call, Mr. Biden "affirmed that the United States stands ready to expand collaboration with Nigeria on issues of common concern, including economic and security matters."

From the foregoing, it would appear there is a strong circumstantial case for the belief by Dr. Goodluck Jonathan and other people who were on the front burner of Nigerian politics, that the Obama administration, for reasons bordering on the Jonathan administration's seeming anti-gay stance, was determined to unseat the Goodluck Jonathan administration as part of its efforts to 'stabilize' Nigeria.

Given the Obama administration's suspected complicity in interfering in Nigeria's Presidential elections of 2015, might it not a bit hypocritical of that same administration to complain of alleged Russian meddling in the 2016 U.S. Presidential election?

Would the Obama administration have taken it kindly if Russian President, Vladimir Putin, had released a broadcast to the American people lecturing them on their civic duties? I think not!

In 2016, Mr. Page left the State Department and moved to Cambridge in the United Kingdom from where he spoke to me. He was adamant that Mr. Babangida Aliyu's version of the events at those meetings where not accurate and was keen to set the records straight. According to Mr. Page, the meetings were attended by twelve Northern governors of whom the most vocal was the then governor of Adamawa state, Admiral Murtala

Nyako. Others at the meetings who voiced anti Jonathan sentiments were then Kano governor, Rabiu Musa Kwankwaso, Aliyu Wammako of Sokoto and Kashim Shettima of Borno. The then governors of Kwara and Kogi were in attendance but were non-committal. Mr. Page noted that the meetings at the United States Institute for Peace were innocuous but that when the governors proceeded to the closed-door sessions at the US State Department, things changed.

According to Mr. Page, present at the State Department meetings were Ambassador Linda Thomas Greenfield who was then the Assistant Secretary of State for African Affairs in the Department of State's Bureau of African Affairs. Also present at the meeting was the then number three man at the State Department, Ambassador Thomas Alfred "Tom" Shannon Jr., acting Deputy Secretary of State of the United States and the Under Secretary of State for Political Affairs.

At that meeting, Admiral Murtala Nyako read out a memo he had written itemizing the case against Jonathan. He was so openly and almost violently against the Jonathan administration in his speech that he had to be openly rebuked at the meeting by the then Nigerian ambassador to the US, Ambassador Adebowale Adefuye of blessed memory. Admiral Nyako's belligerence against the Jonathan administration was so venomous that it prompted a rebuttal from the Gombe state governor, Ibrahim Hassan Dankwambo, who showed loyalty to the then Nigerian President.

According to Mr. Page, this prompted most of the other Northern governors present to turn on him.

In my interview with him, Mr. Page revealed to me that after the anti Jonathan tirades by these governors, they were shepherded to the White House on March 18, 2014 for more meetings. Even though Mr. Page attended the reception at the White House for the Northern governors, he did not make me privy to who were at that particular meeting other than stating that the governors met with then National Security Adviser, Susan Rice. Ms. Rice is however a known Nigerian specialist and was the person who on July 7, 1998, made the tea that the presumed winner of the June 12, 1993 Nigerian Presidential election, chief MKO Abiola, drank minutes before passing away after reportedly foaming at the mouth.

After the meeting, the Obama White House released a statement which said, amongst other things; "Rice and the governors discussed the need to bring an end to the violence and insurgency in northern Nigeria; create broad-based economic opportunity in the north and throughout Nigeria; protect and respect human rights; strengthen democratic governance; and ensure that the 2015 election in Nigeria are free and fair."

What the White House statement did not say, but which I verified from other sources, was that at that meeting, Admiral Nyako accused then President Jonathan of being behind Boko Haram, the Islamic terrorist group that is behind the insurgency in Nigeria's Northeast (the same accusation was publicly made by Nasir El-rufai in 2014. El-rufai was one of a handle of All Progressive Congress party officials that related directly with David Axelrod's firm as AKPD Message and Media prepared the APC for the 2015 elections).

One question arises though, when sub national officials from a nation that is friendly to the United States espouse comments that undermine the President of that friendly nation, why would such persons be honored with very high level meetings that stretched from the State Department to the White House?

When I asked Mr. Page if he thought that the Obama administration was opposed to the re-election of the then Nigerian President, Goodluck Jonathan, he paused and said "my objective opinion is that it was not as if the administration was against Jonathan. There were a few issues. The Obama administration was a bit disappointed (I know that sounds paternalistic) but there were some issues they felt let down on, and you have to remember that the Obama administration supported the transfer of power to Jonathan in 2010. The issues were the human rights situation in the Northeast which has still not changed under Buhari and Diezani Alison-Madueke who they felt should have been removed. There were some issues with some clauses in the Same Sex Marriage (Prohibition) Bill 2013".

Mr. Page continuing said "there were some at the embassy in Nigeria who were actually anti Buhari because of his failure to call his followers to order and stop the post-election violence of 2011".

Although he listed three reasons why the Obama administration felt let down on by Dr. Jonathan, my conversation with Mr. Page gave me a sense that the first two reasons were just excuses and that the main reason was because of the Same Sex Marriage (Prohibition) Bill 2013.

That issue was a deal breaker for the Obama administration because of the strong support they had from the LGBT (Lesbian, Gay, Bisexual or Transgender) community for Mr Obama's re-election campaign of 2012. Per the New York Times, the gay vote was "crucial" to Obama's re-election, whereas to CNN, the LGBT community not only made the difference in 2012 by trooping out to vote for Obama, they were also his top donors.

In Tracy Baim's book, Obama and the Gays: A Political Marriage, she details the influence that the former American President wields with the LGBT community. Very few voting blocs have the get out the vote power that the LGBT community has, being that they are great at organizing for the purpose of advancing their agenda.

I had a firsthand experience of this on April 23, 2016 when I represented Dr. Goodluck Jonathan at a keynote lecture at the California State University in Sacramento. The LGBT community found out that Dr. Jonathan was to speak at the university and organized a protest and a rally against the event which was big enough to attract news coverage from Fox News and when I arrived the event I had to meet with leaders of the LGBT community to persuade them that the Same Sex Marriage (Prohibition) Bill 2013 did not originate from Dr. Jonathan as they erroneously believed, although he signed it as was constitutionally required of him.

There are those that believe that in exchange for their strong support for Obama, they extracted some concessions from him, one of which being to use the full force of his executive powers to advance the course of the LGBT community worldwide, including undermining any foreign government that was perceived to be against same sex marriages and or domestic partnerships.

In fact, after a July 25, 2013 reception at Number 10 Downing Street, held to celebrate the legalization of gay marriage in the United Kingdom, Obama ally and then U.K. Prime Minister, David Cameron, boasted that he was committed to exporting gay marriage around the world. His exact words were 'I am going to export the Bill."

Five months after Cameron made that pledge, Dr. Jonathan, as Nigerian President, signed the Same Sex Marriage (Prohibition) Bill 2013 on January 13, 2014 putting him in direct opposition to both President Obama and Prime Minister Cameron.

Recall that Dr. Jonathan had said "I got on very well with Prime Minister David Cameron but at some point, I noticed that the Americans were putting pressure on him and he had to join them against me."

When I asked him when he felt a change in his relationship with Cameron, former President Jonathan said "sometime in early 2014". Could it be a coincidence that early 2014 is also the same time he signed the law criminalizing same sex marriage in Nigeria? But back to the 2014 meetings, the interesting thing about these meetings is that the Obama administration did not try to balance them out by having other high-level meetings of similar status for governors from Southern Nigeria. Now why would they act this way knowing that Nigeria as a nation was created by amalgamating the two separate nations of Southern Nigeria and Northern Nigeria by the British government in 1914.

Another interesting connection is that these high-level meetings arranged for Northern governors by the Obama administration took place in 2014, at the same time Obama's confidante and former White House Senior Advisor, David Axelrod's firm, AKPD Message and Media, began to work as a paid consultant for the then Nigerian opposition party, All Progressive Congress, which was the vehicle through which incumbent President Muhammadu Buhari rose to power.

Coincidence? You tell me.

Let us connect some more dots.

One of the governors who was most vociferous against Dr. Jonathan at those meetings was Governor Kashim Shettima of Borno state. Bear in mind that he and his colleagues had a closed-door meeting with the then US National Security Adviser, Ms. Susan Rice, on March 18, 2014. Is it a coincidence then that three weeks after Governor Shettima returned from his meeting with Ms. Rice, Boko Haram struck at Chibok town and kidnapped two hundred and seventy six girls at Government Secondary School Chibok? The meeting with Ms. Rice occurred on March 18, 2014, the kidnap of the Chibok girls occurred on April 14, 2014. Prudent minded persons may be wise to take a second look at the Chibok kidnapping.

For starters, for the first three weeks after the kidnapping, the story did not gain traction in the international media, but something unusual happened on May 10, 2014. Every week, President Barack Obama gave a Presidential Address to the US public. On May 10, 2014, for the first time ever, President Obama asked his wife, First Lady Michelle Obama, to deliver the weekly Presidential Address in his stead. The previous week, she had tweeted a picture where she held up a sign that had the hashtag, #BringBackOurGirls. Speaking to the American public, Mrs. Obama said:

"What happened in Nigeria was not an isolated incident. It's a story we see every day as girls around the world risk their lives to pursue their ambitions. "I want you to know that Barack has directed our government to do everything possible to support the Nigerian government's efforts to find these girls and bring them home. In these girls, Barack and I see our own daughters. We see their hopes, their dreams, and we can only imagine the anguish their parents are feeling right now.".

The #BringBackOurGirls hashtag went ballistic and instantly became a cause celebre with music super stars and international celebrities imitating Mrs. Obama's gesture. Why is this piece of information important? Remember that a senior member of the APC boasted publicly that the #BringBackOurGirls movement was 'founded by our members'.

In the next chapter, I dwell on this issue in more detail, but there are still more dots to connect.

The US meetings of Northern governors was arranged by the United States Institute for Peace, with the support of the U.S. State Department's Bureau of Conflict and Stabilization Operations. One of the purposes of the meeting was to discuss "strategies for stabilization and development in northern Nigeria.

Now note that word 'stabilization'. The purpose of that meeting was to hold discussions with Northern governors on how to bring stability to Northern Nigeria amongst other things. On more than one occasion, President Muhammadu Buhari has publicly thanked the Obama administration for its help in the elections that brought him to power. Now note the choice of words that President Buhari used on one of such occasions. On the 20th of July 2015, President Muhammadu Buhari was received by then US President, Barack Obama at the White House. During that meeting, Buhari said: "Nigeria will be ever grateful to President Obama and the United States for making Nigeria consolidate its gains on democracy." President Buhari also said that 'the unrelenting pressure on the immediate past administration by the United States and some European countries made the general elections in Nigeria to be free and fair.'.

Fast forward to the 12th of July, 2016 and President Buhari was playing host to Obama's outgoing ambassador to Nigeria, James F Entwistle, at the Aso Rock Presidential villa. At that meeting, President Buhari said: "The U.S. support before, during and after the 2015 elections was vital to Nigeria's stability and I will never forget the role they played in the stability of Nigeria." Note the use of that word 'stability'.

Notable figures within the US diplomatic circles have for long held the view that Northern Nigeria's absence from the front seat of political power in Nigeria fueled the discontentment that expressed itself in different types of agitations that affect the stability of Nigeria.

Indeed, some have cited the 2010 comments by a notable Northern elder to buttress this view. On October 10, 2010, a Northern elder, Alhaji Lawal Kaita, from the same state (Katsina) as President Muhammadu Buhari said: "The North is determined, if that happens (Jonathan contesting and winning the 2011 election), to make the country ungovernable for President Jonathan or any other Southerner who finds his way to the seat of power on the platform of the PDP against the principle of the party's zoning policy".

When you consider this statement and the meetings that were held with Northern governors leading up to the run up of the 2015 elections by the Obama administration, you begin to understand why that word 'stability' is more than just a word. Also recall that the Obama administration refused to sell weapons to Nigeria and cited the Leahy Law as a hindrance because the law prevents the US from selling weapons to nations whose armies have violated human rights. When Nigeria tried to buy weapons from other nations (most notably Israel), the Obama administration blocked the sale making Nigeria so desperate for weapons that she had to go to the Black Market.

Ironically, just as the Obama administration was refusing to provide support to Nigeria's military in their anti-terror war, the same administration provided major military aid to Chad, Niger and Mali to help their anti-terror war. But according to Amnesty International, all three of these nations (Chad, Niger and Mali) have as bad and in some cases even a worse human rights record than Nigeria. So why were they considered deserving of military aid and support by the Obama administration and Nigeria under Jonathan was not. Thank God the Trump administration has signified its intention to sell weapons to Nigeria. Indeed, the Trump administration has revealed plans to sell 12 Embraer A-29 Super Tucano aircraft with sophisticated targeting gear for nearly $600 million to Nigeria. What has changed? The human rights situation in Nigeria has not improved.

According to an inquiry by the Kaduna state government of Nigeria, in December of 2015 the Nigerian Army slaughtered 347 Shia Muslims many of whom were women and children. There were allegedly state sponsored protests against Amnesty International in March of 2017 because of the organization's report citing that gross human right violations are still occurring in the Northeast.

So rather than the human rights situation improving, it has become worse! The Leahy Law has not changed. It remains on the US statute books.

The ability of the Trump administration to sell weapons to Nigeria despite the Leahy Law proves that the law was used as an excuse to deprive the Jonathan administration of urgently needed weapons to frustrate its anti-terror war and thus affect its popularity. If you think this is far fetched, then consider that, according to the Los Angeles Times, this current sale of weapons to Nigeria by the Trump administration was actually initiated by the Obama administration at the tail end of that government.

Despite the refusal of the Obama administration to sell weapons to Nigeria for the prosecution of Nigeria's anti-terror war against Boko Haram insurgents, Obama sent his Secretary of State, John Kerry, to Nigeria on January 25, 2015, to pressure the Jonathan administration not to postpone the Presidential elections even though he was aware that going ahead with the election on February 14, 2015, at a time when Boko Haram controlled huge swathes of territory, would mean disenfranchising those Nigerians in the Local Government Areas that Boko Haram held in Borno state at that time.

Professor Attahiru Jega, the chairman of the Independent Electoral Commission had said while announcing the postponement of the election that "calling people to exercise their democratic rights in a situation where their security cannot be guaranteed is a most onerous responsibility". To this, Mr. Kerry responded by saying "political interference with the Independent National Electoral Commission is unacceptable and it is critical that the government not use security concerns as a pretext for impeding the democratic process."

How postponing an election, within the time frame allowed by Nigerian law, would mean "impeding the democratic process", when the postponement was done purposely to flush out Boko Haram and allow people who would not have been able to vote had the postponement not taken place was never explained by Mr. Kerry.

Finally, consider the subliminal messages that were communicated by President Obama when he took the unusual step of addressing Nigerians on March 23, 2015 just five days to the presidential elections on March 28, 2019. On that broadcast, Obama told Nigerians: "Now you have an historic opportunity to help write the next chapter of Nigeria's progress by voting in the upcoming elections... Boko Haram wants to destroy Nigeria and all that you have built. By casting your ballot, you can help secure your nation's progress." Note the words 'next chapter'. During the present fourth republic, Nigeria had four successful presidential elections before 2015. 2014 was not a 'next chapter'. The only way it would have been a next chapter would be for the incumbent to be unseated by the opposition. And that, in my opinion, was the subliminal message President Obama was passing across.

Secondly, note the sentence "By casting your ballot you can help secure your nation's progress." When you consider that according to the Los Angeles Times, it was only after the election of Muhammadu Buhari that the Obama administration approved the sale of weapons to Nigeria (which the Trump administration is now implementing), those words by Obama take on a new meaning. Could it be that he was passing on a subliminal message to the Nigerian people that if they were tired of being slaughtered by Boko Haram they were to vote for the right candidate and, voila, the Leahy Law would no longer be a hindrance to the purchase of weapons by Nigeria?

Obama's words appear to have deeper intent when you connect them to the words of his Vice President, Joe Biden. After President Buhari's victory at the polls, then US Vice President, Joe Biden called him to congratulate him. According to the White House transcript of the call, Mr. Biden "affirmed that the United States stands ready to expand collaboration with Nigeria on issues of common concern, including economic and security matters." From the foregoing, it would appear there is a strong circumstantial case for the belief by Dr. Goodluck Jonathan and other people who were on the front burner of Nigerian politics, that the Obama administration, for reasons bordering on the Jonathan administration's seeming anti-gay stance, was determined to unseat the Goodluck Jonathan administration as part of its efforts to 'stabilize' Nigeria. Given the Obama administration's suspected complicity in interfering in Nigeria's Presidential elections of 2015, might it not a bit hypocritical of that same administration to complain of alleged Russian meddling in the 2016 U.S. Presidential election?

Would the Obama administration have taken it kindly if Russian President, Vladimir Putin, had released a broadcast to the American people lecturing them on their civic duties?

I think not!

Chapter 2
HOW TWO KANO GOVERNORS EXPOSED THE ELECTORAL FRAUD OF 2015

Two Governors of Kano state have inadvertently exposed the smoking gun proving that contrary to the Electoral Act, No.6 of 2010 (as amended), foreigners were illegally used to win elections in Kano and other states.

On April 13 2015, then Kano Governor, Rabiu Musa Kwankwaso (now the APC Senator representing Kano Central), speaking live to Channels TV (he cannot claim to have been misquoted in a live video) said, 'Almajiri votes were used to kick Jonathan out of the villa.'

Fast forward to April 7 2017 and the current Governor of Kano, Abdullahi Ganduje, while speaking at the Kaduna Investment Summit said "In Kano, we undertook a survey and we found out that we have more than three million 'almajiris' and 'almajiri' syndrome is one of the serious problems that we have in the North West geopolitical zone. What we discovered from our survey is that many of these 'almajiris' come from Niger Republic, some from Chad, northern Cameroon ".

If according to Kwankwaso, Almajiris were used to win the 2015 elections and if according to Ganduje, most of them are foreigners, it means non Nigerians decided the 2015 elections. This is particularly crucial considering that President Muhammadu Buhari got his highest votes from Kano, Kaduna and Katsina in that order and these are the three states also in that order with the highest number of almajiri!

This is not sour grapes. I am satisfied that the Jonathan era came to an end on May 29, 2015. I have moved on. I run my own business that provides me more income than the salaries of President Muhammadu Buhari's aides. I cannot be more Catholic than a pope who admitted his defeat. This is not about the past, but about the future.

In a postmortem of the 2015 elections it was established that the candidate of the All Progressive Congress, Muhammadu Buhari, won the presidency on the strength of votes from Kano, Katsina, Jigawa and Kaduna which gave him the edge over the candidate of the Peoples Democratic Party, Dr. Goodluck Jonathan.

At the end of the day Buhari polled 15,424,921 to Dr. Jonathan's 12,853,162 votes, defeating the incumbent by about 2,571,759 votes.

In Kano state, the APC candidate polled a total of 1,903,999 votes to the PDP candidates 215,779, a difference of 1,688,220.

In Katsina state, the APC candidate polled a total of 1,345,441 votes to the PDP candidates 98,937, a difference of 1,246,504.

In Kaduna state, the APC candidate polled a total of 1,127,760 votes to the PDP candidates 484,085, a difference of 643,675.

In Jigawa state, the APC candidate polled a total of 885,988 votes to the PDP candidates 142,904, a difference of 743,084.

These four states gave the candidate of the APC a total advantage of 4,321,483 votes over the candidate of the PDP.

Now ask yourself how many of those votes belonged to the foreign almajiri the Governor of Kano confessed to?

Imagine the portends for Nigeria's national security if foreign nationals determine our elections. What about our census figures? What about our National Identity Card Scheme? What about social security?

To put things in perspective, the biggest political issue in the United States today is Russia's alleged influence in the 2016 US Presidential elections in favour of President Donald Trump. Though I do not believe the allegations, the mere suspicion that a foreign and hostile nation may have played a role in swaying the minds of the electorate has given rise to a congressional investigation and dominated the mainstream media.

No nation can claim to be independent if foreigners can influence her choice of leaders which also influences her destiny.

By most reasonable estimates, including figures from the Federal Government itself, there are anywhere from 10 to 12 million almajiri in Northern Nigeria.

For those who do not know what an almajiri is, they are itinerant Islamic scholars under the care of a Malam who teaches them Islamic studies and in return they support the Malam by begging, foraging or by doing odd jobs. In essence, they are the Northern equivalent of the apprenticeship system widely practiced in Southern Nigeria with the one exception that upon finishing their servitude, the Malam does not set them up in business like the apprentice's master is expected to do.

Almajiri are scattered all over Northern Nigeria and if you have not seen them, you need to take a trip up North. There are literally hordes of them in most major Northern cities. Children, youths and adolescents left to their own devices when they are not with their teacher/Malam.

They are vulnerable to the weather and to unscrupulous adults who have often times used them for their own devices. They are often hungry and of course that means that they are often angry. It is very hard to trace their origins because many a times they have lost contact with their parents and extended family.

Indeed, it is easy to agree with Governor Abdullahi Ganduje that many of them are foreigners because our borders are porous, the language spoken around the regions of Niger, Chad and Northern Cameroon is Hausa and the economy of Kano and other major Northern cities attracts immigrants from the poorer areas of those countries.

This is one of the reasons why Northern Nigeria is far more volatile than Southern Nigeria. Because as these almajiri grow up and are unable or unwilling to go back home and are unable or unwilling to find work to support themselves in Northern Nigeria they will become idle and hungry, which is a perfect condition to ignite ethnic, religious and sectarian strife.

Before I go further, I urge my readers to take in the words of no less a person than the Emir of Kano, Muhammadu Sanusi II, coincidentally made a week after the comment by the Governor of Kano.

Emir Sanusi said:

"The majority of technicians in Kano are from the South while untrained indigenes beg. How does that make sense?"

So now, we have foreigners, according to the statements made by the two Kano governors, living as almajiri in Nigeria, voting in Nigeria and quite possibly partaking in the many ethnic, religious and sectarian strife that have engulfed Northern Nigeria at various times.

That is the problem. The question is this: What is the Federal Government doing about this? From my investigation, nothing.

The last time the Federal Government of Nigeria intervened in the life of these almajiri was between 2010 to 2015 when the Jonathan administration set out to build 400 almajiri schools complete with Malam's quarters, laboratories and classrooms to enable Northern Nigeria's almajiris get not just Islamic education, but also Western education and do so under conducive conditions. Eventually, that government succeeded in finishing 165 of such schools.

Ironically, it was the same administration that was trying to help them that they were used to vote out, according to the testimony of Kwankwaso.

What efforts are being made to secure our borders? What efforts are being made to discourage trafficking of children without their parents by persons who want to profit from them through begging or other means? That is not even the worst case scenario.

Imagine that some of these foreign almajiri join our military, police and paramilitary institutions. Who is to stop them? Nigeria does not rely on or have a reliable citizenship database. Anybody who can speak perfect Hausa can claim to be from most states in Northern Nigeria.

What is to prevent foreign born almajiri of non-Nigerian parentage from running for office from the local government level to the highest levels in Nigeria?

In the light of this, it is not impossible and it is even likely that a foreigner could conceivably become President of Nigeria. If a foreigner becomes President of Nigeria, he is not likely to govern with love for Nigerians and may even govern in the lines of a conqueror.

In fact, looking back to some of our most brutal military dictators and their physical features and the strong similarities of their names with names from Niger Republic especially and also Chad and to a lesser extent Northern Cameroon, you and I cannot really swear that a foreigner has not ruled Nigeria in the past!

I will give you an example. Between 1996 and 1999, the President of Niger Republic was a man called Ibrahim Mainassara. That name is almost indistinguishable from a name many Nigerians bare. I have a friend from my youth named Mainassara.

Now it does not stop there. Ibrahim Mainasara, the late President of Niger, was from Dogondoutchi. That word Dogondoutchi is the francophone version of the Hausa word Dogon dutse, meaning high hill (dogon means tall, big, long, or high) (dutse means rock, stone, hill).

You can imagine how easy it is for a Nigerien to pass for a Nigerian and vice verse. In fact, there was a very strong belief in Niger Republic during Mainasara's regime that he was a Nigerian from Argungu in Kebbi state.

Some of us may remember the Maitatsine disturbances that led to tens of thousands of deaths in Northern Nigeria from the late seventies to the mid eighties. These disturbances also led to the destruction of much of ancient city of Yola in present day Adamawa state.

It may surprise many Nigerians that Mohammed Marwa, the founder of that sect which wreaked untold hardship and brought cataclysmic killings and destruction to Nigeria was not even from Nigeria. He was from Marwa, a town in Northern Cameroon.

He came to Nigeria as an itinerant Islamic scholar and gathered a very large following which he turned against the Nigerian state and almost succeeded in destabilizing the Shehu Shagari and the first Muhammadu Buhari regimes.

So entrenched was Mohammad Marwa's maitatsine movement that even after he was killed in 1980, his movement refused to die and his disciple, Musa Makaniki, continued to instigate trouble for Nigeria and when his movement was smashed, he ran for cover in Cameroon until 2004 when he returned to Nigeria and was arrested and tried.

From the above incidences, it is clear that if we do not police our borders and we allow millions of almajiri into our country so they can help us win elections or perform other nefarious roles for us, what happens to national security when they turn on us just like Mohammed Marwa did?

That is a question I leave for the Federal Government that, according to Rabiu Musa Kwankwaso, owes its ascendancy to almajiris, to answer.

Now on to other issues.

On Wednesday the 12th of April 2017, President Muhammadu Buhari did not show up for the regular weekly meetings of the Executive Council of the Federation.

According to Lai Mohammed, President Buhari did not attend the Executive Council of the Federation meeting because he was attending to "other issues"!

If that is Lai's best excuse, then he must really be running out of lies (or lais). It is better for the spokesman to a government not to give any excuse than give such a lame one.

The most important meeting in Nigeria is the Executive Council of the Federation meeting. Leaving Executive Council of the Federation meeting to attend to other issues will be like a CEO leaving a board meeting to attend to visitors. Can such a business thrive? Of course not! No wonder Nigeria is in the shape she is. "Where there is no vision, the people perish"-Proverbs 29:18.

The President must show consistency and stability by attending these meetings regularly. The only excuse that should allow for non attendance of these meetings is when the President is out of the country or when he is ill. Other than that he MUST attend these meetings.

This is why I have always maintained that stability of character is perhaps the most important trait in a leader.

That is why I believe that Politicians who have changed parties multiple times lack the moral authority to condemn prostitutes!

If women who sleep with many men for money are prostitutes why should men who join many political parties for power be called politicians?

That is why I admire Chief Olusegun Obasanjo and Dr. Goodluck Jonathan. Obasanjo is 80 and Jonathan is 59 and in all their time on earth, they have belonged to only one party.

That is a character trait I admire.

Who in the APC has such a character? Not one person. From the President to his cabinet, you can trace their history from APP, to ANPP, to CPC and now to APC. And these are the people that are pontificating today. No wonder Nigeria is so unstable today. How can you have stability with politicians who are not stable?

Let me end this chapter with a quote from Dr. Jonathan's mother, Mrs. Eunice Jonathan who said "Whatever God wants to do with my son, let it be. It is my prayer that the President continues to bring peace to Nigeria and the rest of the world. The president knew that the elections were fraudulent, and people advised him to go to court, but he said no!"

Chapter 3

THE ECONOMY UNDER JONATHAN

Fiction: The Jonathan Administration squandered Nigeria's earnings and did not save, neither did it build infrastructure. It handed over a broke country with broken infrastructure to the Muhammadu Buhari administration.

Fact: Using measurements and assessments from international agencies independent of the Nigerian government, factual evidence establishes, as demonstrated below, that Nigeria had her fastest and largest economic development during the Jonathan years.

Amongst other things, under Jonathan, Nigeria's economy was recalculated during the rebasing of our economy and the nation's Gross Domestic Product was valued at $510 billion (more than twice what it was thought to be). This made Nigeria the largest economy in Africa.

While the rebasing was largely a recalculation of already existing wealth, a good proportion of it was the result of new wealth created by the Jonathan administration and how that wealth was created will be the subject of this chapter amongst other things.

Also, according to the World Health Statistics 2016 published by the World Health Organization, an agency of the United Nations, Average Life Expectancy in Nigeria had increased from 47.4 years when the Jonathan administration came into being in 2010 to above 54 years by the time President Jonathan left office in 2015.

This is the highest level of increase ever recorded in Nigeria since records were kept. However, another study by the Bill and Melinda Gates backed Lancelot Study, as part of a report titled 'Global Burden of Diseases, Injuries and Risk Factors Study' revealed that by their calculations, Average Life Expectancy in Nigeria had actually increased by 11 years over a period of twenty five years with much of that growth coming during the Jonathan years.

How did that administration achieve such a feat? This chapter will also address that.

When I asked former President Jonathan what he thought led to the present sorry state of the Nigerian economy today, he responded thus:

"When I look back at the avalanche of criticism, I shudder at the extent we are willing to go in the direction of distortion to hit a political goal. I was watching President Obama on CNN, asking the Republicans not to talk the American economy down in order to reach the White House. I listened to President Muhammadu Buhari tell a congregation that Nigeria's economy was one of the fastest rising economies in the world. But the economy was gone during the campaigns. APC campaigners tore the Nigerian economy to shreds by mouth, while shying away from mouthing "the largest economy on the continent". It was also one of the fastest rising economies before the new administration came. We must have done something in office after all. May be we were not as clueless as they campaigned. It is a lesson I hope would be learnt. If you embark on digging a hole for your enemy, you better make it shallow, because you might end up in the hole yourself. How do you talk back all the investors you already told that all was lost?"

On the 23rd of January, 2015, CNN Money, a globally recognized expert agency projected that with the rate of economic growth experienced by Nigeria during the Jonathan years (7%), Nigeria was projected to be the third fastest growing economy in the world for 2015.

This is just as the United Nations Conference on Trade and Development (UNCTAD) rated Nigeria under Jonathan as the number 1 destination for Foreign Direct Investment in Africa in 2013.

The policies that led to this feat will also be explored in this chapter.
The Economy:

The Jonathan administration left $2.07 billion in the Excess Crude Account when it handed over to the Buhari administration on May 29, 2015 as well as Foreign reserves of$29.6 billion. Slightly over $5 billion was left for the Buhari administration by way of dividend payments from the Nigerian Liquefied Natural Gas Company.

At the time of the handover, Nigeria's GDP growth rate was 6.1% (for the last full year before the handover), inflation rate was at single digit and stood at 9.5%, the Naira to Dollar exchange rate stood at $1 to NGN199 and at the parallel market it was $1 to NGN216. In the same period, the Jonathan administration maintained a debt to GDP ratio of 11%.

Under Jonathan, the percentage of non-performing loans in the banking sector fell to just 5%, one of the best rates in the world, just as Nigeria's stock market capitalization increased to .13.23 trillion. These are verifiable indicators of a very sound economy.

The price of premium motor Spirit (also known as petrol) stood at .87, the price of a 25kg bag of rice (a staple food in Nigeria) was 8,000.

The International Food Policy Research Institute had listed Nigeria under President Jonathan as one of only a handful of nations to have reduced hunger levels (Nigeria's hunger index dropped from 16.3 in 2005 to 15 in 2013).

The administration took concrete steps to reduce unemployment. One of such steps was the Graduate Internship Programme through which 46,000 graduates were paired with firms and businesses to gain experience, with the Federal Government paying their wages for the period of their internship.

Another such program was the Youth With Innovation in Nigeria, YouWIN initiative which was a business plan competition opened to Nigerian youths by which they sent in their business proposal to a non-governmental evaluating body which selected the best proposals for purposes of training the winners and giving them grants of between $12,000 and $100,000.

Altogether, 3,600 youth entrepreneurs benefited from this program which had the multiplier effect of creating 80,000 jobs.

This is even as hundreds of Nigerian youths benefited from the Presidential Special Scholarship Scheme For Innovation And Development to study at the best universities around the world.

As a result of the Nigerian Oil and Gas Industry Content Development Bill 2010, otherwise known as the Local Content Law, which then President Jonathan signed into law, indigenous participation in the oil industry grew.

As a direct result of that law, Shell Petroleum Development Corporation awarded a $50 million pipeline development contract to a Nigerian firm, SCC Nigeria limited, the first that such a contract has even been awarded locally.

Also because of that law, Nigerian owned marine vessels increased from 54 to 338, an expansion which led to the creation of 30,000 new jobs in that industry.

The Jonathan administration is also credited with reviving Nigeria's previously moribund railways and is responsible for the ability of Nigerians to affordably crisscross the length and breadth of their county. In 2011, the railway passenger traffic in was 1 million people per annum, by 2015 it had increased 5-fold to over 5 million people per annum.

As a result of the policies of that administration, Nigeria's telecommunications industry grew to the point of contributing 8.53% to GDP by 2014, up from 0.62% in 2001.

As a result of the grants given to Nollywood by the Jonathan administration (no other government before or after Jonathan has given grants to Nollywood) the Nigerian film industry expanded and was contributing 1.4% to Nigeria's GDP when Jonathan left office in 2015.

In the health sector, Nigeria, under President Jonathan successfully eradicated polio and guinea worm infestation and was certified by the United Nations (although polio resurfaced in 2016, AFTER Jonathan had left office), this is even as infant and maternal mortality rate dropped from 704 per 100,000 live births in 1990 to half that number by 2015 when that administration handed over the baton to the succeeding administration.

Based on the above, any objective observer must conclude that the Jonathan administration left Nigeria on a sound macroeconomic footing when it handed over power to its successor administration.

On the issue of savings, I have addressed the issue of the solid reserves left by the Jonathan administration. Now let us address the issue of the Excess Crude Account which is the account most cited in accusations against the previous administration when issues of not saving come up.

John Burroughs once said "a man can fail many times, but he is not a failure until he begins to blame somebody else"?

Those words should be embossed on a plaque and placed in a very prominent location somewhere where all Nigerian politicians can see it.

Seeing this admonition regularly may help members of the political class take responsibility and stop acting the victim.

Those in the habit of noising about the 'alternative fact' that the Jonathan administration did not save up during the sunny days for the rainy day, should not l forget so soon that the Jonathan administration met $6.5 billion in the Excess Crude Account upon inception in 2010 and increased it to almost $9 billion by 2012.

However, the Nigerian Governors Forum, using their influence at the House of Representatives, had gotten that body to declare the Excess Crude Account illegal in 2012.

So excruciating was the pressure from the Nigerian Governors Forum and most notably from the then Rivers state Governor, Rotimi Amaechi, (now the minister of transport) for the Jonathan administration to end the Excess Crude Account and the Sovereign Wealth Fund regimes and instead share the funds in those accounts amongst the three tiers of government that they approached the Supreme Court, to challenge the legality of the Excess Crude Account and then President Jonathan's decision to transfer $1 billion from that account to the Sovereign Wealth Fund.

In fact, after hosting a meeting of the forum on September 21, 2012, at the Rivers state Governor's lodge, Rotimi Amaechi said inter alia:

"On the Excess Crude Account, Forum unanimously decided to head back to Court to enforce the Federal Government's adherence to the constitution."

To those who do not know what the Constitution says, let me give you an insight by quoting from Section 162.

Section 162, provides that

"(1) The Federation shall maintain a special account to be called 'the Federation Account' into which shall be paid all revenues collected by the Government of the Federation, except the proceeds from the personal income tax of the personnel of the Armed Forces of the Federation, the Nigeria Police Force, the Ministry or department of government charged with responsibility for Foreign Affairs and the residents of the Federal Capital Territory, Abuja.

"(2) The President, upon the receipt of advice from the Revenue Mobilisation Allocation and Fiscal Commission, shall table before the National Assembly proposals for revenue allocation from the Federation Account, and in determining the formula, the National Assembly shall take into account, the allocation principles especially those of population, equality of States, internal revenue generation, land mass, terrain as well as population density;

"(3) Any amount standing to the credit of the Federation Account shall be distributed among the Federal and State Governments and the Local Government Councils in each State on such terms and in such manner as may be prescribed by the National Assembly."

From the above it was clear what the Amaechi led Governor's forum wanted.

Mr. Amaechi led the governors in taking the Federal Government to court. The Jonathan administration offered an out of courts settlement with the governors in a deal that would have seen the federal government sharing some of the money and saving up the rest for Nigeria's future but the governors rejected the offer.

In fact, the Jonathan Administration had argued at the Supreme Court that sharing the money in the ECA would affect "the day to day running of the nation's economy".

Working in tandem with Mr. Amaechi and his supporters in the Nigerian Governors Forum, the then minority APC members of the House of Representatives approached a Federal High Court on the 7th of February, 2014, for a perpetual injunction restraining the Jonathan administration from operating the ECA and to pay all the proceeds of that account into the Federation Account for sharing amongst the three tiers of government.

As a result of these actions, the Jonathan administration paid the 36 states of the federation a total of N2.92 trillion from the Excess Crude Account between 2011 and 2014. That is over US$20 billion using the value of the Naira at that time.

So, it is quite clear that anyone who accuses the Jonathan administration of not saving for the rainy day has not been told the whole story.

Infrastructure and Projects

On Tuesday, the 26th of July, 2016, President Muhammadu Buhari commissioned the $1.457 billion Abuja-Kaduna standard gauge rail project. This was a project built and COMPLETED by the Jonathan administration.

It is a 187-kilometer railway that enables Nigerians to live in Kaduna and work in Abuja.

That administration also remodeled all the nation's 22 federally owned airports and for the first time covered the entire country with radar coverage via the Total Radar Coverage of Nigeria Project (TRACON) which led to Nigeria receiving category 1 status (the highest status achievable) by the US Department of Transportation.

The Jonathan administration also built 12 federal universities in Katsina, Zamfara, Yobe, Nasarawa, Kogi, Taraba, Gombe, Jigawa, Kebbi, Ebonyi, Bayelsa and Ekiti states.

By building 12 new federal universities and 165 almajiri schools and renovating 507 additional secondary schools all over Nigeria through the Universal Basic Education Commission, the Jonathan administration not only increased access to education, the policy also had the intended side effect of putting hundreds of thousands of youths to work which stimulated the economy and contributed to GDP growth.

There is no state in Nigeria that did not benefit from the Jonathan administration because the main goal of the developmental efforts of that government was inclusivity.

While not an exhaustive list of what that administration did, below follows a summary of some of the projects implemented by the Federal Government between 2010 and 2015.

In Abia, Jonathan completed and commissioned Phase 1 of the 504MW Alaoji Power Station and built sub power stations in Aba, Mbalano, Ohafia and Okigwe even as he reconstructed and reopened Ohafia barracks to stem kidnapping. He rehabilitated and reopened the NNPC depot at Aba after 6years of closure. He rehabilitated the Aba-Owerri road and the Umuahia-Bende-Uhuafia road. In addition, he developed the inland container depot in Isialangwa.

In the Federal Capital Territory of Abuja, Jonathan built, completed and Commissioned Phases 3 and 4 Lower Usuma Dam Water Treatment Plants, completed the 10 lane Kubwa-Abuja Expressway and expanded the Airport Expressway to 10 lanes. He established the Nigerian Centre for Disease Control and built a laboratory for that institution in Gadua, Abuja. He also completed the Federal Staff Hospital in Jabi, completed the Trauma Center at the National Hospital Abuja and the Abuja Teaching Hospital in Gwagwalada.

In Adamawa State, Jonathan constructed 5 Almajiri schools and the Nigerian Air force Comprehensive Secondary School and renovated the Yola airport and added an additional terminal at that facility. He also built power substations at Mubi, Song, and Gulak. This is even as he completed the Yola-Numan road.

In Anambra State, Jonathan completed Onitsha River Port, repaired Onitsa-Owerri Road and kick started the process of the 2nd Niger Bridge. He also added three additional lanes to the Onitsha Head Bridge up to Iweka Junction. He also built an Aircraft Maintenance School at Akili – Ozuzo, in Ogbaru Local Government Area and funded ecological projects including the Nanka/Oko Landslide Project, the Nkisi Water Works and the Okpolo/Ire Ojoto Erosion Control Project. The Jonathan administration also rehabilitated the Nnamdi Azikwe University Teaching Hospital Nnewi.

In Akwa Ibom State, Jonathan established a new Federal Polytechnic in Ukana and the Nkari Earth dam and rehabilitated FG roads. He also constructed a 100,000 metric tonnes capacity silos and constructed three MDG/NDE skill Acquisition centers in each of the three Senatorial Districts ofAkwa Ibom.

In Bauchi State, Jonathan equipped the Abubakar Tafawa Balewa Teaching Hospital Bauchi and built multiple Almajiri schools. He also set up the Cancer Treatment Centre at the Abubakar Tafawa Balewa Teaching Hospital, Bauchi and reconstructed the Yashi – Basher – Dengi road section in Bauchi and Plateau States and Rehabilitated the Futuk – Yalo Road. The Jonathan government also established a model nomadic education centre in Bauchi and constructed a 510-seater lecture hall in the Federal Polytechnic, Bauchi.

In Benue State, Jonathan substantially advanced the Loko-Oweto bridge and completed the Makurdi Water Supply Scheme supplying to 1 million people. He also rehabilitated the Lafia – Makurdi Road and the Aliade to Uturkpo Road and constructed a Perishable Cargo Terminal at the Makurdi Airport. This is even as he constructed a new library at the Federal Government College Otobi, Benue state.

In Borno State, Jonathan fought desertification with the Great Green Wall Project and rehabilitated the Uba – Mbalala Road. He dualized the Maiduguri-Kano road. He also set up the Presidential Initiative for the Northeast and the Victims Support Fund which raised ₦59 billion for the Northeast.

In Cross River State, Jonathan rehabilitated the Margaret Ekpo International Airport and modernized the University of Calabar Teaching Hospital. He also performed Land Reclamation and Erosion control works project in Essien town – Ekorinim community. This is even as he constructed an Agricultural Skills Training Centre in the state.

In Delta State, Jonathan took Itakpe-Ajaokuta-Warri railway to 80% completion and kick started the $16B Gas City Project at Ogidigben. He also rehabilitated the Warri Refinery and its access roads. This is even as he built new library projects at the Federal Government College (FGC) Warri and the Federal Government Girls College Ibusa and completed the Capital dredging of the Lower River Niger from Warri (Delta state) to Baro (Niger State) a total of 532 kilometers. His government also established the Nigerian Maritime University and the NIMASA Shipyard and Dockyard at Okerekoko.

In Ebonyi State, Jonathan established the Federal University in Ndufe – Alike, repaired over 250km of roads and built power substations. He also rehabilitated the 43 KM Obiozara – Uburu – Ishiagu Road and the 37Km Oji – Achi Obeagu – Maku – Awgu – Ndeabor – Mpu – Okpanku – Akaeze

Road. This even as he constructed a one-storey hostel, a class room building and a procurement building at the Federal Government Girls College Ezembo, Ebonyi State. The Jonathan administration also established the National Obstetric Fistula Centre at Abakiliki and established a national cancer screening center within.

In Edo State, Jonathan completed the Ihovbor power Station, reconstructed the BeninOre-Sagamu and equipped the University of Benin Teaching Hospital. He also performed the emergency reinstatement of washout/gully erosion at KM 127 + 000 at Auchi along Okene – Benin road and 14 + 000 Km along Auchi-Agenebode Road. This is even as he constructed water supply projects in Northern Ishan of Edo State (9million litres per day plant capacity) for Uromi, Ubiaja, Ugengu, Igueben and Ugboha and built multiple jetties at Agenebode. The administration also performed land reclamation and erosion control works project at Igonton – Igbanke and Iyom/Okhelen – Awo road Uromi.

In Ekiti State, Jonathan established the Federal University in Oye – Ekiti, and rehabilitated Ekon – Alaaye – Erinmo – Iwaraja road in Ekiti and Osun States and Omuo – Ifaki road of Ado – Ilumoba – Agbado Ikare Akoko Road sections A & B.

In Enugu State, Jonathan gave the South East their first International Airport and revived the Port Harcourt-Enugu rail line. He also upgraded facilities at the University of Nigeria Teaching Hospital, Enugu, leading to the resumption of Open Heart Surgeries at that facility. He also constructed the ₦2.57 Billion Dam Project in Adada River Dam to provide Portable Water, Electricity and Irrigation for agriculture activities and the Ada Rice Irrigation Project at Uzo – Uwani and another irrigation facility at Amagunze Rice Product farm, Enugu. This is even as he constructed the Export Crop Preservation and Conditioning Centre in Enugu State. He also implemented the "Mmutu Bu Ike" back-to-school program which was targeted at reducing the high number of out-of-school children.

In Gombe State, Jonathan established the Federal University in Kashere and built multiple Almajiri schools. He also reinstated the collapsed section of Gombe – Potiskum road and rehabilitated the Gombe – Numan – Yola Road (Section II).

In Imo State, Jonathan rehabilitated the Sam Mbakwe International Airport and completed power stations and built sub stations. The administration also commenced but did not finish building the Oguta port. He also constructed an administrative complex and Entrepreneurial Studies Complex at the Federal University of Technology Owerri (FUTO). The Jonathan government constructed a new Federal High Court Owerri division complex and established and constructed buildings for a Court of Appeal Division in Owerri. Not done, that regime completed the 14Km Mbaise – Ngwa Road with a bridge at Imo/ Abia State. The Jonathan administration also advanced work at the Egbema power station.

In Jigawa State, Jonathan established the Federal University in Dutse, built multiple Almajiri schools and multiple silos. He also constructed 15 Rows of Green Belt(80Km) via the Presidential Initiative on Afforestation Program. That administration constructed a block of laboratories in Jigawa State Polytechnic, Dutse.

In Kano State, Jonathan revived the Lagos-Kano rail, built multiple Almajiri schools, renovated the Malam Aminu Kanu International Airport and built silos. He also rehabilitated and upgraded the Nigerian Police Academy in Wudil to University Status. The Jonathan administration dualized the Kano/ Maiduguri road and rehabilitated the Kano-Katsina road. This is even as the Jonathan administration project of an 80 Km, 15–row Green Belt via the Presidential Initiative on Afforestation benefited Kano and ten other Northern border states.

In Kaduna State, Jonathan completed the Standard Gauge Kaduna-Abuja rail that enables you work in Abuja and live in Kaduna. He also revived the Zaria/Kaura Namoda rail route. Completed Galma multi-purpose Dam which will be commissioned by the present administration. The Jonathan administration also built multiple almajiri schools in Kaduna and rehabilitated the access road to the Kaduna refinery.

In Katsina State, Jonathan established the Federal University in Dutsin-ma, built 5 Almajiri schools and multiple silos. He rehabilitated the Umaru Yar'Adua International Airport Katsina and established the Wind Energy Generation Farm. He also rehabilitated the Kano-Kazaure-Daura-Mai Adua roads.

In Kebbi State, Jonathan established the Federal University in Kalgo, built multiple Almajiri schools and multiple silos. He also set up a CBN cash office in Kebbi and the Federal Radio Corporation of Nigeria (FRCN) built an FM station in the state.

In Kogi State, Jonathan established the new Federal University in Lokoja, and completed and commissioned the Geregu power plant. He dualized the 212 Km Lokoja – Abuja Road, Lokoja Okene – Benin Road and completed the Aladja – Ajaukuta Rail line and constructed a federal high court building in the state.

In Kwara State, Jonathan revived Jebba-Kano and Ilorin–Offa rail lines, built Almajiri schools and made progress on but did not complete the ongoing reconstruction of the Ibadan-Ilorin road. He also rehabilitated the Ilorin International Airport and through the Education Trust Fund, the Jonathan Government granted the University of Ilorin .4.2 Billion in 2012 for the University of Ilorin Geological Research and Resort Centre at Aran – Orin as well as for a new faculty of Arts and Faculty of Education, Multi – Purpose hall and a central Research Laboratory and the automation of the University of Ilorin Library.

In Lagos State, Jonathan revived the Lagos-Kano rail, introduced intercity air conditioned diesel trains and rehabilitated Murtala Mohammed International Airport. He also upgraded facilities at the Lagos University Teaching Hospital, leading to the first successful Open Heart Surgeries and first kidney transplant surgery at that facility.

In Nasarawa State, Jonathan established a new Federal University in Lafia and rehabilitated the Lafia–Makurdi road as well as the Lafia – Doma road, Lafia – Obi – Awe Road, Nasarawa – Karsh – Ara roads and constructed the Karshi bypass. Through the Tertiary Education Trust Fund (TetFund) President Jonathan's administration constructed the Faculty of Arts Lecture theatre at the Nasarawa State University Keffi as well as the construction of the faculty of Administration lecture theatre, Faculty of Social Science lecture theatre and construction of an Academic staff office complex. He also constructed a Cancer Treatment Centre at the Federal Medical Centre Keffi and built 3 MDG/NDE Skill Acquisition Centres in each of the three Senatorial Districts of Nasarawa state.

In Niger State, Jonathan dredged River Niger up to Baro, Baro Port at 95% completion, and commenced building the Zungeru power plant on which work is ongoing. He dualized the Suleja – Minna Road and built the Umar Yar'Adua Hospital for highway emergency response and built multiple almajiri schools. He also equipped Mathematics and Chemistry Laboratories at the Federal Government Academy, Suleja and established a Maritime Institute at the Ibrahim Badamasi Babangida University, Lapai.

In Ondo State, Jonathan completed and commissioned the 500 MWs Omotosho Power Plant Phase 2 and renovated the Akure airport. He also rehabilitated the Akure – Ilesa express way and advanced work on the Erusu/ Arigidi Dam in Akoko North West Area of Ondo State under the Benin – Owena River Basin Development Authority (BORBDA). The Jonathan government, knowing the importance of education to Ondo state also established a new federal Polytechnic at Ile – Oluji and constructed MDG/NDE Skill Acquisition Centres in each of the 3 Senatorial districts of Ondo State as well as constructed Jetties at Igbokoda.

In Ogun State, Jonathan rehabilitated the Sagamu-Ore road as well as the Ijebu Igbo Ajegunle–Araromi–Ife-SekonaRoad(SectionII).He also completed and commissioned the 750mw Olounshogo power station built through the Niger Delta Power Holding Company of Nigeria.

In Osun State, Jonathan re-equipped OAUTH, constructed silos, built power substations, repaired Efon Alaaye-Erinmo Ijesha-Iwarga road. He also built the 32 million cubic capacity Ilesha Water Dam Project that provides drinking and irrigation water for the state.

In Oyo State, Jonathan reconstructed (not repaired) Lagos-Ibadan Rd and has commenced constructing the Lag-Ibadan hi-speed rail. He also upgraded facilities at the University College Hospital, Ibadan, leading to the resumption of Open Heart Surgeries at that facility. The Jonathan administration kick started the Lagos – Ibadan new gauge Rail Line Service and upgraded the former Liberty stadium and renamed it the Obafemi Awolowo stadium to honor the late Founding father and former Premier of the Western Region and rehabilitated the Ibadan Airport. He also reconstructed the Gbogan – Iwo Road and rehabilitated the Old Oyo – Ogbomosho Road and the Odo oba – Takie – Gambari otte road.

In Plateau State, Jonathan completed the reconstruction of the Vom-Manchok road, construction of earth dam in Heipang and power substations. He also constructed the Faculty of Social Science, Faculty of Post Graduate Studies, International Conference Centre and hostels in University of Jos through the TETFund and rehabilitated the railway lines from Kuru Station in Plateau state to Bauchi station as well as advanced work on the Barkin Ladi Dam. That regime constructed a Perishable Cargo Terminal at the Jos airport and completed the Mangu Water Treatment Plant and supply scheme which provides 10 million litres per day and serves Gundiri and Mangu townships in Plateau state.

In Rivers State, Jonathan revived the Port Harcourt-Enugu Rail line, Rehabilitated the Port Harcourt International Airport and upgraded University of Port Harcourt Teaching Hospital. He also established a Cancer Treatment Centre at the University of Port Harcourt Teaching Hospital and created a new Federal Oil and Gas Polytechnic in Bonny.

In Sokoto State, Jonathan fought desertification with the Great Green Wall and built multiple Almajiri schools. He rehabilitated the Shagari irrigation Project and the Sokoto airport even as it began constructing the nation's largest hajj terminal in the same airport and rehabilitated the Funtua – Gusau – Sokoto Road. He also commissioned the special baby intensive care unit and officers' quarters at ABUTH.

In Taraba State, Jonathan established the Federal University in Wukari and constructed the Kashimbila Multi-Purpose Dam Project. He also rehabilitated the Wukari – Takum Road, Wukari /Akwana Road and made progress in the construction of the Jalingo – Kuna Lau Road (Section II) even as he built multiple silos in the state.

In Yobe State, Jonathan established Federal University of Gashua, Almajiri schools & Gashua–Hadejia 132KV double circuit transmission line.

In Zamfara State, Jonathan established the Federal University Gusau, built multiple Almajiri schools and constructed silos. He also rehabilitated the Funtua-Gusau-Sokoto road and the Namoda Jiba Road Section IV. In addition, the administration established a cancer treatment centre at the Federal Medical Centre Gusau, and rehabilitated the Bakalori irrigation and hydro-power project.

Again, these are not an exhaustive list of the projects and infrastructural accomplishments of the Jonathan administration. This just serves to disprove the argument that the administration did not develop infrastructure or develop the nation. Indeed, it is my considered opinion that in terms of projects, no previous or present administration has come close to achieving what the Jonathan administration achieved for Nigeria.

If anyone feels otherwise, he is challenged to come forward with facts.

The Jonathan administration left $2.07 billion in the Excess Crude Account when it handed over to the Buhari administration on May 29, 2015 as well as Foreign reserves of$29.6 billion. Slightly over $5 billion was left for the

Buhari administration by way of dividend payments from the Nigerian Liquefied Natural Gas Company. At the time of the handover, Nigeria's GDP growth rate was 6.1% (for the last full year before the handover), inflation rate was at single digit and stood at 9.5%, the Naira to Dollar exchange rate stood at $1 to NGN199 and at the parallel market it was $1 to NGN216. In the same period, the Jonathan administration maintained a debt to GDP ratio of 11%.

Under Jonathan, the percentage of non-performing loans in the banking sector fell to just 5%, one of the best rates in the world, just as Nigeria's stock market capitalization increased to ₦13.23 trillion. These are verifiable indicators of a very sound economy. The price of premium motor Spirit (also known as petrol) stood at ₦87, the price of a 25kg bag of rice (a staple food in Nigeria) was ₦8,000. The International Food Policy Research Institute had listed Nigeria under President Jonathan as one of only a handful of nations to have reduced hunger levels (Nigeria's hunger index dropped from 16.3 in 2005 to 15 in 2013). The administration took concrete steps to reduce unemployment. One of such steps was the Graduate Internship Programme through which 46,000 graduates were paired with firms and businesses to gain experience, with the Federal Government paying their wages for the period of their internship.

Another such program was the Youth With Innovation in Nigeria, YouWIN initiative which was a business plan competition opened to Nigerian youths by which they sent in their business proposal to a non-governmental evaluating body which selected the best proposals for purposes of training the winners and giving them grants of between $12,000 and $100,000. Altogether, 3,600 youth entrepreneurs benefited from this program which had the multiplier effect of creating 80,000 jobs. This is even as hundreds of Nigerian youths benefited from the Presidential Special Scholarship Scheme For Innovation And Development to study at the best universities around the world.

As a result of the Nigerian Oil and Gas Industry Content Development Bill 2010, otherwise known as the Local Content Law, which then President Jonathan signed into law, indigenous participation in the oil industry grew. As a direct result of that law, Shell Petroleum Development Corporation awarded a $50 million pipeline development contract to a Nigerian firm, SCC Nigeria limited, the first that such a contract has even been awarded locally. Also because of that law, Nigerian owned marine vessels increased from 54 to 338, an expansion which led to the creation of 30,000 new jobs in that industry. The Jonathan administration is also credited with reviving Nigeria's previously moribund railways and is responsible for the ability of Nigerians to affordably crisscross the length and breadth of their county. In 2011, the railway passenger traffic in was 1 million people per annum, by 2015 it had increased 5-fold to over 5 million people per annum.

As a result of the policies of that administration, Nigeria's telecommunications industry grew to the point of contributing 8.53% to GDP by 2014, up from 0.62% in 2001. As a result of the grants given to Nollywood by the Jonathan administration (no other government before or after Jonathan has given grants to Nollywood) the Nigerian film industry expanded and was contributing 1.4% to Nigeria's GDP when Jonathan left office in 2015. In the health sector, Nigeria, under President Jonathan successfully eradicated polio and guinea worm infestation and was certified by the United Nations (although polio resurfaced in 2016, AFTER Jonathan had left office), this is even as infant and maternal mortality rate dropped from 704 per 100,000 live births in 1990 to half that number by 2015 when that administration handed over the baton to the succeeding administration. Based on the above, any objective observer must conclude that the Jonathan administration left Nigeria on a sound macroeconomic footing when it handed over power to its successor administration.

On the issue of savings, I have addressed the issue of the solid reserves left by the Jonathan administration. Now let us address the issue of the Excess Crude Account which is the account most cited in accusations against the previous administration when issues of not saving come up. John Burroughs once said "a man can fail many times, but he is not a failure until he begins to blame somebody else". Those words should be embossed on a plaque and placed in a very prominent location somewhere where all Nigerian politicians can see it. Seeing this admonition regularly may help members of the political class take responsibility and stop acting the victim. Those in the habit of noising about the 'alternative fact' that the Jonathan administration did not save up during the sunny days for the rainy day, should not forget so soon that the Jonathan administration met $6.5 billion in the Excess Crude Account upon inception in 2010 and increased it to almost $9 billion by 2012. However, the Nigerian Governors Forum, using their influence at the House of Representatives, had gotten that body to declare the Excess Crude Account illegal in 2012. So excruciating was the pressure from the Nigerian Governors Forum and most notably from the then Rivers state Governor, Rotimi Amaechi, (now the minister of transport) for the Jonathan administration to end the Excess Crude Account and the Sovereign Wealth Fund regimes and instead share the funds in those accounts amongst the three tiers of government that they approached the Supreme Court, to challenge the legality of the Excess Crude Account and then President Jonathan's decision to transfer $1 billion from that account to the Sovereign Wealth Fund.

In fact, after hosting a meeting of the forum on September 21, 2012, at the Rivers state Governor's lodge, Rotimi Amaechi said inter alia: "On the Excess Crude Account, Forum unanimously decided to head back to Court to enforce the Federal Government's adherence to the constitution." To those who do not know what the Constitution says, let me give you an insight by quoting from Section 162. Section 162, provides that "(1) The Federation shall maintain a special account to be called 'the Federation Account' into which shall be paid all revenues collected by the Government of the Federation, except the proceeds from the personal income tax of the personnel of the Armed Forces of the Federation, the Nigeria Police Force, the Ministry or department of government charged with responsibility for Foreign Affairs and the residents of the Federal Capital Territory, Abuja. "(2) The President, upon the receipt of advice from the Revenue Mobilisation Allocation and Fiscal Commission, shall table before the National Assembly proposals for revenue allocation from the Federation Account, and in determining the formula, the National Assembly shall take into account, the allocation principles especially those of population, equality of States, internal revenue generation, land mass, terrain as well as population density; "(3) Any amount standing to the credit of the Federation Account shall be distributed among the Federal and State Governments and the Local Government Councils in each State on such terms and in such manner as may be prescribed by the National Assembly." From the above it was clear what the Amaechi led Governor's forum wanted. Mr. Amaechi led the governors in taking the Federal Government to court. The Jonathan administration offered an out of courts settlement with the governors in a deal that would have seen the federal government sharing some of the money and saving up the rest for Nigeria's future but the governors rejected the offer. In fact, the Jonathan Administration had argued at the Supreme Court that sharing the money in the ECA would affect "the day to day running of the nation's economy". Working in tandem with Mr. Amaechi and his supporters in the Nigerian Governors Forum, the then minority APC members of the House of Representatives approached a Federal High Court on the 7th of February, 2014, for a perpetual injunction restraining the Jonathan administration from operating the ECA and to pay all the proceeds of that account into the Federation Account for sharing amongst the three tiers of government. As a result of these actions, the Jonathan administration paid the 36 states of the federation a total of N2.92 trillion from the Excess Crude Account between 2011 and 2014. That is over US$20 billion using the value of the Naira at that time.

So, it is quite clear that anyone who accuses the Jonathan administration of not saving for the rainy day has not been told the whole story. Infrastructure and Projects On Tuesday, the 26th of July, 2016, President Muhammadu Buhari commissioned the $1.457billion Abuja-Kaduna standard gauge rail project. This was a project built and COMPLETED by the Jonathan administration. It is a 187-kilometer railway that enables Nigerians to live in Kaduna and work in Abuja. That administration also remodeled all the nation's 22 federally owned airports and for the first time covered the entire country with radar coverage via the Total Radar Coverage of Nigeria Project (TRACON) which led to Nigeria receiving category 1 status (the highest status achievable) by the US Department of Transportation. The Jonathan administration also built 12 federal universities in Katsina, Zamfara, Yobe, Nasarawa, Kogi, Taraba, Gombe, Jigawa, Kebbi, Ebonyi, Bayelsa and Ekiti states. By building 12 new federal universities and 165 almajiri schools and renovating 507 additional secondary schools all over Nigeria through the Universal Basic Education Commission, the Jonathan administration not only increased access to education, the policy also had the intended side effect of putting hundreds of thousands of youths to work which stimulated the economy and contributed to GDP growth.

There is no state in Nigeria that did not benefit from the Jonathan adminis-tration because the main goal of the developmental efforts of that government was inclusivity. While not an exhaustive list of what that administration did, below follows a summary of some of the projects implemented by the

Federal Government between 2010 and 2015. In Abia, Jonathan completed and commissioned Phase 1 of the 504MW Alaoji Power Station and built sub power stations in Aba, Mbalano, Ohafia and Okigwe even as he reconstructed and reopened Ohafia barracks to stem kidnapping. He rehabilitated and reopened the NNPC depot at Aba after 6years of closure. He rehabilitated the Aba-Owerri road and the Umuahia-Bende-Uhuafia road. In addition, he developed the inland container depot in Isialangwa. In the Federal Capital Territory of Abuja, Jonathan built, completed and Commissioned Phases 3 and 4 Lower Usuma Dam Water Treatment Plants, completed the 10 lane Kubwa-Abuja Expressway and expanded the Airport Expressway to 10 lanes. He established the Nigerian Centre for Disease Control and built a laboratory for that institution in Gadua, Abuja. He also completed the Federal Staff Hospital in Jabi, completed the Trauma Center at the National Hospital Abuja and the Abuja Teaching Hospital in Gwagwalada. In Adamawa State, Jonathan constructed 5 Almajiri schools and the Nigerian Air force Comprehensive Secondary School and renovated the Yola airport and added an additional terminal at that facility. He also built power substations at Mubi, Song, and Gulak. This is even as he completed the Yola-Numan road. In Anambra State, Jonathan completed Onitsha River Port, repaired Onitsa-Owerri Road and kick started the process of the 2nd Niger Bridge. He also added three additional lanes to the Onitsha Head Bridge up to Iweka Junction. He also built an Aircraft Maintenance School at Akili – Ozuzo, in Ogbaru Local Government Area and funded ecological projects including the Nanka/Oko Landslide Project, the Nkisi Water Works and the Okpolo/Ire Ojoto Erosion Control Project. The Jonathan administration also rehabilitated the Nnamdi Azikwe University Teaching Hospital Nnewi. In Akwa Ibom State, Jonathan established a new Federal Polytechnic in Ukana and the Nkari Earth dam and reha-bilitated FG roads. He also constructed a 100,000 metric tonnes capacity silos and constructed three MDG/NDE skill Acquisition centers in each of the three Senatorial Districts of Akwa Ibom. In Bauchi State, Jonathan equipped the Abubakar Tafawa Balewa Teaching Hospital Bauchi and built multiple Almajiri schools. He also set up the Cancer Treatment Centre at the Abubakar Tafawa Balewa Teaching Hospital, Bauchi and reconstructed the Yashi – Basher – Dengi road section in Bauchi and Plateau States and Rehabilitated the Futuk – Yalo Road. The Jonathan government also established a model nomadic education centre in Bauchi and constructed a 510-seater lecture hall in the Federal Polytechnic, Bauchi. In Benue State, Jonathan substantially advanced the Loko-Oweto bridge and completed the Makurdi Water Supply Scheme supplying to 1 million people. He also rehabilitated the Lafia – Makurdi Road and the Aliade to Uturkpo Road and constructed a Perishable Cargo Terminal at the Makurdi Airport. This is even as he constructed a new library at the Federal Government College Otobi, Benue state. In Borno State, Jonathan fought desertification with the Great Green Wall Project and rehabilitated the Uba – Mbalala Road. He dualized the Maiduguri-Kano road. He also set up the Presidential Initiative for the Northeast and the Victims Support Fund which raised .59 billion for the Northeast. In Cross River State, Jonathan rehabilitated the Margaret Ekpo International Airport and modernized the University of Calabar Teaching Hospital. He also performed Land Reclamation and Erosion control works project in Essien town – Ekorinim community.

This is even as he constructed an Agricultural Skills Training Centre in the state. In Delta State, Jonathan took Itakpe-Ajaokuta-warri railway to 80% completion and kick started the $16B Gas City Project at Ogidigben. He also rehabilitated the Warri Refinery and its access roads. This is even as he built new library projects at the Federal Government College (FGC) Warri and the Federal Government Girls College Ibusa and completed the Capital dredging of the Lower River Niger from Warri (Delta state) to Baro (Niger State) a total of 532 kilometers. His government also established the Nigerian Maritime University and the NIMASA Shipyard and Dockyard at Okerekoko. In Ebonyi State, Jonathan established the Federal University in Ndufe – Alike, repaired over 250km of roads and built power substations. He also rehabilitated the 43 KM Obiozara – Uburu – Ishiagu Road and the 37Km Oji – Achi Obeagu – Maku – Awgu – Ndeabor – Mpu – Okpanku – Akaeze Road. This even as he constructed a one-storey hostel, a class room building and a procurement building at the Federal Government Girls College Ezembo, Ebonyi State. The Jonathan administration also established the National Obstetric Fistula Centre at Abakiliki and established a national cancer screening center within. In Edo State, Jonathan completed the Ihovbor power Station, reconstructed the BeninOre-Sagamu and equipped the University of Benin Teaching Hospital. He also performed the emergency reinstatement of washout/gully erosion at KM 127 + 000 at

Auchi along Okene – Benin road and 14 + 000 Km along Auchi-Agenebode Road. This is even as he constructed water supply projects in Northern Ishan of Edo State (9million litres per day plant capacity) for Uromi, Ubiaja, Ugengu, Igueben and Ugboha and built multiple jetties at Agenebode. The administration also performed land reclamation and erosion control works project at Igonton – Igbanke and Iyom/Okhelen – Awo road Uromi. In Ekiti State, Jonathan established the Federal University in Oye – Ekiti, and rehabilitated Ekon – Alaaye – Erinmo – Iwaraja road in Ekiti and Osun States and Omuo – Ifaki road of Ado – Ilumoba – Agbado Ikare Akoko Road sections A & B. In Enugu State, Jonathan gave the South East their first International Airport and revived the Port Harcourt-Enugu rail line. He also upgraded facilities at the University of Nigeria Teaching Hospital, Enugu, leading to the resumption of Open Heart Surgeries at that facility. He also constructed the .2.57 Billion Dam Project in Adada River Dam to provide Portable Water, Electricity and Irrigation for agriculture activities and the Ada Rice Irrigation Project at Uzo – Uwani and another irrigation facility at Amagunze Rice Product farm, Enugu. This is even as he constructed the Export Crop Preservation and Conditioning Centre in Enugu State. He also implemented the "Mmutu Bu Ike" back-to-school program which was targeted at reducing the high number of out-of-school children. In Gombe State, Jonathan established the Federal University in Kashere and built multiple Almajiri schools. He also reinstated the collapsed section of Gombe – Potiskum road and rehabilitated the Gombe – Numan – Yola Road (Section II). In Imo State, Jonathan rehabilitated the Sam Mbakwe International Airport and completed power stations and built sub stations. The administration also commenced but did not finish building the Oguta port. He also constructed an administrative complex and Entrepreneurial Studies Complex at the Federal University of Technology Owerri (FUTO). The Jonathan government constructed a new Federal High Court Owerri division complex and established and constructed buildings for a Court of Appeal Division in Owerri. Not done, that regime completed the 14Km Mbaise – Ngwa Road with a bridge at Imo/ Abia State. The Jonathan administration also advanced work at the Egbema power station. In Jigawa State, Jonathan established the Federal University in Dutse, built multiple Almajiri schools and multiple silos. He also constructed 15 Rows of Green Belt(80Km) via the Presidential Initiative on Afforestation Program.

That administration constructed a block of laboratories in Jigawa State Polytechnic, Dutse. In Kano State, Jonathan revived the Lagos-Kano rail, built multiple Almajiri schools, renovated the Malam Aminu Kanu International Airport and built silos. He also rehabilitated and upgraded the Nigerian Police Academy in Wudil to University Status. The Jonathan administration dualized the Kano/Maiduguri road and rehabilitated the Kano-Katsina road. This is even as the Jonathan administration project of an 80 Km, 15–row Green Belt via the Presidential Initiative on Afforestation benefited Kano and ten other Northern border states. In Kaduna State, Jonathan completed the Standard Gauge Kaduna-Abuja rail that enables you work in Abuja and live in Kaduna. He also revived the Zaria/Kaura Namoda rail route. Completed Galma multi-purpose Dam which will be commissioned by the present administration. The Jonathan administration also built multiple almajiri schools in Kaduna and rehabilitated the access road to the Kaduna refinery. In Katsina State, Jonathan established the Federal University in Dutsin-ma, built 5 Almajiri schools and multiple silos. He rehabilitated the Umaru Yar'Adua International Airport Katsina and established the Wind Energy Generation Farm. He also rehabilitated the Kano-Kazaure-Daura-Mai Adua roads.

In Kebbi State, Jonathan established the Federal University in Kalgo, built multiple Almajiri schools and multiple silos. He also set up a CBN cash office in Kebbi and the Federal Radio Corporation of Nigeria (FRCN) built an FM station in the state. In Kogi State, Jonathan established the new Federal University in Lokoja, and completed and commissioned the Geregu power plant. He dualized the 212 Km Lokoja – Abuja Road, Lokoja Okene – Benin Road and completed the Aladja – Ajaukuta Rail line and constructed a federal high court building in the state. In Kwara State, Jonathan revived Jebba-Kano and Ilorin–Offa rail lines, built Almajiri schools and made progress on but did not complete the ongoing reconstruction of the Ibadan-Ilorin road. He also rehabilitated the Ilorin International Airport and through the Education Trust Fund, the Jonathan Government granted the University of Ilorin ₦4.2 Billion in 2012 for the University of Ilorin Geological Research and Resort Centre at Aran – Orin as well as for a new faculty of Arts and Faculty of Education, Multi – Purpose hall and a central Research Laboratory and the automation of the University of Ilorin Library. In Lagos State, Jonathan revived the Lagos-Kano rail, introduced inter-city air conditioned diesel trains and rehabilitated Murtala Mohammed International Airport. He also upgraded facilities at the Lagos University Teaching Hospital, leading to the first successful Open Heart Surgeries and first kidney transplant surgery at that facility. In Nasarawa State, Jonathan established a new Federal University in Lafia and rehabilitated the Lafia–Makurdi road as well as the Lafia – Doma road, Lafia – Obi – Awe Road, Nasarawa – Karsh – Ara roads and constructed the Karshi bypass. Through the Tertiary Education Trust Fund (TetFund) President Jonathan's adminis-tration constructed the Faculty of Arts Lecture theatre at the Nasarawa State University Keffi as well as the construction of the faculty of Administration lecture theatre, Faculty of Social Science lecture theatre and construction of an Academic staff office complex. He also constructed a Cancer Treatment Centre at the Federal Medical Centre Keffi and built 3 MDG/NDE Skill Acquisition Centres in each of the three Senatorial Districts of Nasarawa state. In Niger State, Jonathan dredged River Niger up to Baro, Baro Port at 95% completion, and commenced building the Zungeru power plant on which work is ongoing. He dualized the Suleja – Minna Road and built the Umar Yar'Adua Hospital for highway emergency response and built multiple almajiri schools. He also equipped Mathematics and Chemistry Laboratories at the Federal Government Academy, Suleja and established a Maritime Institute at the Ibrahim Badamasi Babangida University, Lapai.

In Ondo State, Jonathan completed and commissioned the 500 MWs Omotosho Power Plant Phase 2 and renovated the Akure airport. He also rehabilitated the Akure – Ilesa express way and advanced work on the Erusu/ Arigidi Dam in Akoko North West Area of Ondo State under the Benin – Owena River Basin Development Authority (BORBDA). The Jonathan government, knowing the importance of education to Ondo state also established a new federal Polytechnic at Ile – Oluji and constructed MDG/NDE Skill Acquisition Centres in each of the 3 Senatorial districts of Ondo State as well as constructed Jetties at Igbokoda. In Ogun State, Jonathan rehabilitated the Sagamu-Ore road as well as the Ijebu Igbo Ajegunle–Araromi–Ife-Sekona Road (Section II). He also completed and commissioned the 750mw Olounshogo power station built through the Niger Delta Power Holding Company of Nigeria. In Osun State, Jonathan re-equipped OAUTH, constructed silos, built power substations, repaired Efon Alaaye-Erinmo Ijesha-Iwarga road. He also built the 32 million cubic capacity Ilesha Water Dam Project that provides drinking and irrigation water for the state. In Oyo State, Jonathan reconstructed (not repaired) Lagos-Ibadan Rd and has commenced constructing the Lag-Ibadan hi-speed rail. He also upgraded facilities at the University College Hospital, Ibadan, leading to the resumption of Open Heart Surgeries at that facility. The Jonathan administration kick started the Lagos – Ibadan new gauge Rail Line Service and upgraded the former Liberty stadium and renamed it the Obafemi Awolowo stadium to honor the late Founding father and former Premier of the Western Region and rehabilitated the Ibadan Airport. He also reconstructed the Gbogan – Iwo Road and rehabilitated the Old Oyo – Ogbomosho Road and the Odo oba – Takie – Gambari otte road. In Plateau State, Jonathan completed the reconstruction of the Vom-Manchok road, construction of earth dam in Heipang and power substations. He also constructed the Faculty of Social Science, Faculty of Post Graduate Studies, International Conference Centre and hostels in University of Jos through the TETFund and rehabilitated the railway lines from Kuru Station in Plateau state to Bauchi station as well as advanced work on the Barkin Ladi Dam. That regime constructed a Perishable Cargo Terminal at the Jos airport and completed the Mangu Water Treatment Plant and supply scheme which provides 10 million litres per day and serves Gundiri and Mangu townships in Plateau state. In Rivers State, Jonathan revived the Port Harcourt-Enugu Rail line, Rehabilitated the Port Harcourt International Airport and upgraded University of Port Harcourt Teaching Hospital. He also established a Cancer Treatment Centre at the University of Port Harcourt Teaching Hospital and created a new Federal Oil and Gas Polytechnic in Bonny. In Sokoto State, Jonathan fought desertification with the Great Green Wall and built multiple Almajiri schools. He rehabilitated the Shagari irrigation Project and the Sokoto airport even as it began constructing the nation's largest hajj terminal in the same airport and rehabilitated the Funtua – Gusau – Sokoto Road. He also commissioned the special baby intensive care unit and officers' quarters at ABUTH. In Taraba State, Jonathan established the Federal University in Wukari and constructed the Kashimbila Multi-Purpose Dam Project. He also rehabilitated the Wukari – Takum Road, Wukari /Akwana Road and made progress in the construction of the Jalingo – Kuna Lau Road (Section II) even as he built multiple silos in the state. In Yobe State, Jonathan established Federal University of Gashua,

Almajiri schools & Gashua–Hadejia 132KV double circuit transmission line. In Zamfara State, Jonathan established the Federal University Gusau, built multiple Almajiri schools and constructed silos. He also rehabilitated the Funtua-Gusau-Sokoto road and the Namoda Jiba Road Section IV. In addition, the administration established a cancer treatment centre at the Federal Medical Centre Gusau, and rehabilitated the Bakalori irrigation and hydro-power project. Again, these are not an exhaustive list of the projects and infrastructural accomplishments of the Jonathan administration. This just serves to disprove the argument that the administration did not develop infrastructure or develop the nation. Indeed, it is my considered opinion that in terms of projects, no previous or present administration has come close to achieving what the Jonathan administration achieved for Nigeria. If anyone feels otherwise, he is challenged to come forward with facts.

Chapter 4
THE TRUTH ABOUT CHIBOK GIRLS

Fiction: The Jonathan Administration did not do anything to rescue thekidnapped Chibok girls.

This allegation has been made chiefly by the new Nigerian administration and it is not very clear if it is borne out of willful ignorance or mischief, but whatever the case, the fact remains that this allegation is simply not true.

Let me state, for the benefit of conspiracy theorists that I was able to trace some Chibok Girls now living in the United States and from their testimony, it is clear beyond a shadow of a doubt that there was a kidnap of a large number of girls from of Government Girls Secondary School Chibok. There is no doubt about that. The incident is real, it happened, it is a historical fact.

According to Patience Bulus and Mercy Paul who were students of Government Girls Secondary School Chibok and were there on that day Boko Haram terrorists came calling at their school with a trailer. They could not identify what type of trailer it was beyond saying that it was similar to the type used by the Dangote Group. The Dangote Group generally uses trucks manufactured by China's Sinotruk and they are heavy trucks and trailers that certainly have the capacity to carry 276 girls.

According to Patience and Mercy, they were initially told by the terrorists that they were there to rescue them. One of their leaders asked in the Hausa language, 'what are you doing in this school'? It was a rhetorical question. Mercy and Patience were both in that truck but jumped down, at great risk to themselves, while it was moving en-route to Sambisa Forest. Boko Haram's hideout.

When asked why most of the Chibok Girls could not speak in passable English even though they were meant to be writing a physics examination, Patience revealed that most young people in Chibok communicated in Hausa and that though their teachers tried to teach them in English at school, they communicated more in Hausa even while at school.

The girls are now taking their General Educational Development tests in a school in the East Coast of the United States.

Now that we have established that the incident did indeed take place, is there any truth to the accusation against the Jonathan administration that it did "nothing" to rescue the kidnapped girls?

Several efforts were made by the Jonathan Administration to secure the release of the Chibok girls as the factual and verifiable timelines below will show, but some of those efforts were frustrated by the then opposition led All Progressive Congress state government and massive propaganda efforts by the party at the national and international level which resulted in mistrust and fed the suspicion that there is a conspiracy whose components would be revealed after the APC state government of Borno state led by Governor Kashim Shettima might have left office in 2019.

Other actions and omissions included in the timelines will also help the reader independently connect the dots between cause and effect in this whole saga.

Timelines:

March 12, 2014: The then minister of state for education, Mr. Nyesom Wike, wrote the Governors of Borno, Yobe and Adamawa and advised them not to hold the West African Senior Secondary Certificate Examinations in areas susceptible to the Boko Haram insurgency. This letter, with reference number HMSE/FME/147/VOL.1/150 and titled: 'Security challenges and the conduct of the 2014 WASSCE and SSCE in Borno, Yobe and parts of Adamawa States'.*

The Governors of Yobe and Adamawa acknowledged the letter and cooperated with the then Peoples Democratic Party led Federal Government to bus students to secure locations to write their scheduled school leaving examinations.

April 14, 2014: Contrary to the advice given by the PDP led Federal Government of President Goodluck Jonathan, the APC led Government of Governor Kashim Shettima, for reasons best known to it, chose to ignore that advise and held the WASSCE examinations in Chibok, a mainly Christian town that was susceptible to attacks from the Islamic extremist group, Boko Haram. On the day in question, the girls of Government Girls Secondary School Chibok were kidnapped by Boko Haram while preparing to write their final physics examinations.

Curiously, both the Principal of the school and her two Vice Principals were not on the school's campus and the girls were locked inside a dormitory. Where were the matrons? Where were the hostel mistresses? Where were the other senior staff of the school?

The Principal of the school, Hadjiya Asabe Kwambura, a Muslim, later claimed to have gone to Maiduguri for a 'medical check-up' on the day of the abduction. It seemed very inauspicious for a principal of a school to schedule a non-emergency 'medical check-up' for a time when the school she presided over was having perhaps its most important activity of the year, school leaving examinations. It seemed as the girls were meant to be sitting ducks.

This same woman later changed her story when she told Fox News that she had gone to Maiduguri, the capital of Borno state, to buy medicines and was informed by her daughter about the kidnap. But how did her daughter, a Muslim and a student of the school, avoid being kidnapped?

It is noteworthy that this principal was never reprimanded or disciplined or in any way made to take responsibility for this obvious dereliction of duty by the Borno state government who runs the school.

Flash forward to April 2, 2016:Governor Kashim Shettima confessed in an interview with Premium Times that he, the chief security officer of the state, DID NOT inform then President Jonathan when the girls were kidnapped for reasons best known to him.

April 17, 2014: Exactly three days after the kidnap, President Jonathan who had only been made aware of the issue by the army and not by the state government (because of the deliberate refusal of the APC led government of Borno state to brief him) called for an emergency meeting at the Presidential villa.

Multiple dates in April, 2004:The military, principally the air force, were given conflicting information as to what direction the fleeing terrorists took when they captured the girls. Were these conflicting information a deliberate effort to send the military on a wild goose chase?

Flash Forward to January 6, 2017: One of the Chibok girls who escaped from her captors granted an interview to the New York Times and revealed that they were not taken to Sambisa Forest by the terrorists as previously thought. According to her testimony, they were rather taken to the Borno state capital of Maiduguri and kept at a house there for months.

Flash Forward to January 11, 2017: Chibok Community leader, Pastor

Bulus Baba, in an interview with local media corroborated the New York Times report and said even after they left Maiduguri they were moved to another town and kept in the home of an influential local politician. According to him:

"The girls said, they spent over 8 months in Gwoza local government area along with other abducted women. They said they were kept at a resident of one of the top politicians in that local government area until at a point when a fighter jet dropped bomb that touch part of the house killing some of the girls."

Flash Forward to 26 December, 2016: The British Broadcasting Corporation revealed that the Chibok girls that had either escaped from their captors or been released as a result of a swap deal with the new APC Federal Government have been prevented from meeting their families or from talking with the press.

According to the BBC:

The freed girls have been in government custody since their release but were brought home to Chibok for Christmas.

But family members told the BBC that the girls were kept in a politician's house and barred from going home. They were also prevented from attending church services with their families. The girls were taken to the house of an assembly member in Chibok to be reunited with their parents but weren't allowed to go to their own homes. "I can't believe my daughter has come this close to home but can't come home," said one father. "There's no point bringing them to Chibok only to be locked in another prison. They couldn't even go to church on Christmas Day."

The above reports show an eerie similarity with the way the girls were, according to their own testimony, treated immediately after their abduction by Boko Haram (they were taken to Maiduguri and to Gwoza and kept in the home of a top politician).

May 2, 2014: Then President Jonathan sets up a fact-finding mission to determine the facts of the kidnap and stressed that the mission's work would not interfere with search and rescue efforts.

May 2, 2014: Frustrated by the school's authorities to come clean with accurate information about the identities of the missing girls, the Christian Association of Nigeria released the names of the kidnapped girls for the first time.

May 3, 2014: Charles Eguridu, head of the West African Examination Council's National Office in Nigeria revealed in a testimony broadcast live on national television that WAEC had asked the Borno state Governor not to hold examinations at Chibok due to safety issues, but that Governor Shettima, in writing, had assured WAEC that he would provide adequate security for Chibok, a promise he did not keep. According to Mr. Eguridu: "The Borno state government also refused to relocate the students from Chibok to safer places like Maiduguri. "Borno state government only agreed to relocate the remaining 189 pupils after the abduction of the girls."
Talk about medicine after death.

May 4, 2014: After consistent confused and contradictory information from the Borno state Government and various other authority figures, the Presidency invited the principal actors in the Chibok saga to the Presidential villa to ascertain the truth. The Presidency was shocked at the non-appearance of officials of the Borno state government. The governor's wife who was invited shunned the event and when the then First Lady, Dame Patience Jonathan saw the scanty representation from Borno she famously exclaimed 'na only you waka come'?

May 5, 2014: Many residents of Gamboru Ngala were killed by Boko Haram forces after troops stationed there left that town to go to the Sambisa forest to look for the missing girls. The precision behind the arrival of Boko Haram just as the troops left the town gave rise to strong suggestions that the terrorists were tipped off by a mole.

May 6, 2014: The then National Publicity Secretary of the APC and now the current minister of information, Lai Mohammed, released a statement calling the Presidency's intervention a 'distraction'.

May 6, 2014: In response to a request by the Nigerian Government for help, then United States President, Barack Obama announced that the US was dispatching personnel into the area to help search for the missing girls.

May 9, 2014: Nigeria welcomed experts from the United States and the United Kingdom to help search for the girls.

May 11, 2014: Borno state Governor, Kashim Shettima tells the local and international media the girls had "been sighted". In view of later testimony by the released girls that they had initially been kept in Maiduguri, Shettima's accounts now elicit more suspicion especially as Boko Haram released a video a day after the revelation by Governor Shettima.

May 12, 2014: Boko Haram releases a video purporting to be of the Chibok girls. However, in that video, the girls do not look terrified and one of them is shown distracted as she appears to be sending a text or making a call on her mobile phone which was visible to the camera. This video is still publicly available on YouTube. Giving the testimony that they were held in Maiduguri the state capital before being taken to Gwoza, how could this video have been shot in day light without attracting some attention?

May 26, 2014: The Nigerian military, through its Chief of Defence Staff, Air Marshal Alex Badeh, revealed that it knew the location of the girls but could not attack because of fear of loss of lives of the girls after a similar operation in Sokoto to save an Italian and a Briton led to loss of lives of the hostages taken by an affiliate of Boko Haram.

Unspecified Date in May 2014: The Jonathan administration began secret negotiations to secure the release of the Chibok girls.

September 7, 2014: In an interview with foremost Northern Nigeria daily, Leadership Newspaper, some of the parents of the kidnapped girls alleged that the entire saga was a conspiracy against the mostly Christian community by the school officials who were, surprisingly, overwhelmingly Muslim. In that interview, a Chibok parent, Bulama Jonah, said:

"We still believe that there was an internal collaboration in the abduction of our daughters by the Boko Haram gunmen, because we have correct information that some of the teachers, who are very senior in the school, managed to move their own daughters and family out of the school premises before the attack. "That is why we are insisting that (the Borno state) government must provide our daughters and we would not take it lightly if they don't produce our girls for us. The girls were in their custody, because school premises belong to government; and we believe they were aware of the attack but failed to provide security for them."

October 6, 2014: Then President Jonathan visits Niamey as part of efforts to secure the release of the Chibok girls with the help of the Nigerien government.

October 15, 2014: During the Presidential Declaration by then candidate Muhammadu Buhari, now the incumbent President, Audu Ogbeh, at that time the Director General of the campaign (he was later replaced) said on live Television that the pressure group Bring Back our Girls, led by a virulent critic of the Jonathan administration, Oby Ezekwesili, is led by "members of our party, the APC." This is an exact quote and reflects the politicization of the saga.

Flash Forward to July 12, 2016: President Muhammadu Buhari appoints Bring Back our Girls co-founder, Ms. Hadiza Bala Usman, as the head of Nigeria's largest and perhaps most profitable parastatal, the Nigerian Ports Authority. Many consider this as a reward to Ms. Usman and a corroboration of the "members of our party, the APC" comment of Chief Audu Ogbeh.

October 17, 2014: A truce was announced with Boko Haram after negotiations which was to allow for the release of the Chibok girls. The truce was broken by Boko Haram who reneged on their promise to release their captives.

May 5, 2017: 82 Chibok girls were released by Boko Haram to the Nigerian government after negotiations that involved a prisoner swap and payments: But questions about this incidence remain.

On May 3, 2017, international news syndicate, AFP, reported that on Friday April 29, 2017 fighter jets from the Nigerian Airforce had pounded Boko Haram positions in Balla village, which is 25 miles) from Damboa, just outside Sambisa Forest. Citing intelligence reports, they reported that the bombing was so intense that several Boko Haram fighters were killed including the group's deputy leader, Abba Mustapha, alias Malam Abba and another leader, Abubakar Gashua, alias Abu Aisha, described as a key person in the group's hierarchy.

The Nigerian Air force released a statement in support of these reports on the same day and said "Battle damage assessment conducted after the strike showed that several leaders of the Boko Haram terrorist organisation and their followers were killed during the attacks".

Babakura Kolo, a member of the Civilian JTF (a militia registered with the Nigerian government to help in the fight with Boko Haram) testified that "a number of commanders were killed."

On May 4, 2017, Boko Haram's leader, Abubakar Shekau, releases a video denouncing and taunting the Nigerian government over the attack and promising reprisals.

Yet, after this incident on April 29 that led to the death of their top commanders and many of their foot soldiers, Boko Haram still went on the release 82 Chibok girls to the same Nigerian government that their leader had sworn revenge on exactly a week later? Does this add up? Does this gel with reality? Does this even make sense?

On May 7, 2017, when the girls were ferried over to the Nigerian Presidential

Villa at Aso Rock, Abuja to meet with President Muhammadu Buhari photographs released showed them looking very well fed and robust. In fact, the next day (May 8) Africa's top blog, Linda Ikeji's blog published a photo of the released girls side by side with a picture of a woman and her baby in one of the Internally Displaced Persons camp in Borno state for a side by side comparison and these Chibok girls, who had been living rough inside Sambisa forest looked well fed and buxom while the woman in the IDP camp looked haggard and hungry. How is this possible?

From the above timelines and factual details, it would seem obvious to an objective reader that there is more to the abduction than meets the eye. Things do not quite add up and the more things are meant to be cleared up the opaquer they get.

Indeed, on May 18, 2016, Ryan Cummings, a security analyst who has been consulted by Time Magazine, CNN and AFP published that there "may be slightly more" to the Chibok saga than meets the eye!

In fact, nothing encapsulates the situation better than the fact that ever since members of the APC who had founded the Chibok Advocacy group Bring Back our Girls, left the group, the APC led Federal Government which had shown great tolerance and support for the group became increasingly intolerant of the group to the extent that the headline of the Northern Flagship paper, Daily Trust, read 'FG Cautions BBOG Over Criticism'.

Alas, the APC, the then opposition that once joined the group to criticize the PDP led administration of President Jonathan, now cautions same group not to try the same with them!

May 5, 2017: 82 Chibok girls were released by Boko Haram to the Nigerian government after negotiations that involved a prisoner swap and payments: But questions about this incidence remain. On May 3, 2017, international news syndicate, AFP, reported that on Friday April 29, 2017 fighter jets from the Nigerian Airforce had pounded Boko Haram positions in Balla village, which is 25 miles) from Damboa, just outside Sambisa Forest. Citing intelligence reports, they reported that the bombing was so intense that several Boko Haram fighters were killed including the group's deputy leader, Abba Mustapha, alias Malam Abba and another leader, Abubakar Gashua, alias Abu Aisha, described as a key person in the group's hierarchy.

The Nigerian Air force released a statement in support of these reports on the same day and said "Battle damage assessment conducted after the strike showed that several leaders of the Boko Haram terrorist organisation and their followers were killed during the attacks".

Babakura Kolo, a member of the Civilian JTF (a militia registered with the Nigerian government to help in the fight with Boko Haram) testified that "a number of commanders were killed."

On May 4, 2017, Boko Haram's leader, Abubakar Shekau, releases a video denouncing and taunting the Nigerian government over the attack and promising reprisals.

Yet, after this incident on April 29 that led to the death of their top commanders and many of their foot soldiers, Boko Haram still went on the release 82 Chibok girls to the same Nigerian government that their leader had sworn revenge on exactly a week later? Does this add up? Does this gel with reality? Does this even make sense?

On May 7, 2017, when the girls were ferried over to the Nigerian Presidential Villa at Aso Rock, Abuja to meet with President Muhammadu Buhari photographs released showed them looking very well fed and robust. In fact, the next day (May 8) Africa's top blog, Linda Ikeji's blog published a photo of the released girls side by side with a picture of a woman and her baby in one of the Internally Displaced Persons camp in Borno state for a side by side comparison and these Chibok girls, who had been living rough inside Sambisa forest looked well fed and buxom while the woman in the IDP camp looked haggard and hungry. How is this possible?

This is not the first time Chibok girls have been released. Almost exactly a year ago, just a week before the current Nigerian administration marked its first year in office some Chibok girls were also released. Another batch were released in October 2016. The thing is that when these girls are released there is a media blackout on them. No one is allowed near them to interview them.

I understand that they have gone through an ordeal, but Malala also went through a similar or even worse ordeal and no one shielded her from the press. Malala Yousafzai was shot at age 15 by the Taliban and left unconscious. She survived and she was threatened by the Taliban who threatened to kill her should they catch her. Her case was one of clear and present danger. Yet she was not sequestered from the public even though, like the Chibok girls, her English was not so good at first. In fact, an international press tour was arranged for her, placing her on the world stage and kick starting the activism that earned her a Nobel Prize making her the youngest person ever to be so awarded.

One would have thought that is what would have played out for the released girls.

Last October, 21 Chibok girls were release by Boko Haram after negotiations. Till date, these girls have been kept from the press. Even their own parents are not allowed access to them according to a New York Times piece on them published on March 11, 2017. The girls are kept in safe house according to the New York Times. During the Christmas holidays, they were allowed to visit Chibok but were housed in the home of a "top politician". Their parents were only allowed to 'visit them'. Soldiers guarded the girls and after some hours asked the parents of the girls to leave.

On Christmas Day itself, they were denied entry to the politician's house to see their own children and on January 8, 2017 the girls were returned to their safe house and according to the New York Times "Neither the public nor their parents have been able to see them since."

No one really knows what went on with these girls since their abduction. It is all smoke and mirrors.

These girls are innocent. They did not kidnap themselves. They were pawns in a game whose puppeteers we do not yet know. No one should raise any questions about these girls after what they have been through. But surely, we can raise questions about events themselves. Think people. Am I the only one seeing this?

And one thing puzzles me, and that is the fact that ever since members of the APC who had founded the Chibok Advocacy group Bring Back our Girls left the group, the APC led Federal Government which had shown grate tolerance and support for the group became increasingly intolerant of the group to the extent that the headline of the Northern Flagship paper, Daily Trust, read 'FG Cautions BBOG Over Criticism'.

Alas, the opposition group that once joined them to criticism the PDP led administrations of President Jonathan now cautions them not to try the same with them!

I began this chapter with the story of Patience and Mercy. Mercy is very shy and reserved, but when asked what her future ambition is, she states that she wants to get the best education the United States can offer and then return home to contest for Nigeria's Presidency! What a wonderful outlook. Despite her ordeal, she still has a positive outlook. To me, this is the best story coming out of Chibok and I very much wish that Providence would pave the way for Mercy to achieve her dreams.

Chapter 5
THE RESURGENCE OF NIGER DELTA MILITANCY

Fiction: Dr. Goodluck Jonathan is behind the resurgence of militancy in the Niger Delta

Fact: The attempt to smear the reputation of former President Goodluck Jonathan by raising suspicion through sponsored articles that he is behind the recent resurgence of militancy in the Niger Delta is unfortunate. That the same hastily cooked up lies were reported simultaneously and almost word for word by client media of the powers that be is evidence of the fact that someone powerful is out to get the former President.

Nigerians and the international community know Dr. Goodluck Jonathan as a man of peace. He is also noted for his peaceful nonviolent political philosophy, aptly captured in the Jonathan Doctrine of peace, briefly summarized in his oft repeated quote "my political ambition is not worth the blood of any Nigerian".

This quote was further expanded on December 11, 2014 when Dr. Goodluck Jonathan said, "Nobody's political ambition is worth the blood of any Nigerian".

Not only did he utter these words, but Dr. Jonathan lived them. He was probably one of the most criticized President in Nigeria's history, yet he did not arrest even one critic and is noted for being the President that signed the Freedom of Information Act into law to promote freedom of speech and freedom after the speech.

And during the height of the Niger Delta militancy between 2007 and 2009, it was precisely then Vice President Goodluck Jonathan that used his influence to persuade Niger Delta militants to drop their weapons and embrace peace leading to the Niger Delta Amnesty that was announced by President Umar Musa Yar'adua on June 26, 2009.

The Presidential Amnesty Program was a brainchild of Dr. Goodluck Jonathan and is one of the world's most successful peace initiatives and it was only successful because Dr. Jonathan's character as a man of peace was well known within the Niger Delta specifically and Nigeria in general.

Despite an attempt on his life and the bombing of his country home by militants in 2007, Dr. Jonathan's bravery in going to the militants' camp without any security in 2009 to reason with them to give up the militancy is the only reason Nigeria's oil output increased from 700,000 Barrels Per Day in 2009 to over two million Barrels Per Day thereafter.

Would Dr. Jonathan now use his own hand to destroy what he has built?

Let us even consider the reports in themselves. One of the conjectures used by the propagators of this lie to pull the wool over the eyes of Nigerians and the international community is contained in this quote "It has been known in government circles that Jonathan may be behind the Niger Delta Avengers. The speed with which he denied the allegation spoke volumes."

This quotation was reported by various media as emanating from a faceless member of the present administration's intelligence infrastructure.

There has never been such a childish and amateurish justification for sullying the hard-earned reputation for peace of a man like former President Jonathan as this. In fact, Dr. Goodluck Jonathan does not have a reputation for peace, in truth, he has a character of peace.

When in November of 2012 Boko Haram named Major General Muhammadu Buhari (rtd), now the current President of Nigeria, as one of its chosen mediators he quickly and immediately denied and rejected his nomination by Boko Haram.

Flowing from the same warped reasoning, his speedy denial is also evidence that he had a hand in the terrorism occasioned by the radical Islamic sect, but we know that is not true because Boko Haram tried to kill Mr. Buhari.

If it were that Dr. Jonathan did not quickly and completely deny any links with the Niger Delta Avengers and any other militant groups, then those behind this wishy-washy story would have changed their tactics and would have said that his non-denial is evidence of his complicity.

Another so called evidence used against the former President in this sponsored report is the fact that he called for peace and urged militants not to declare a republic or contemplate secession.

In the disturbed thinking of the sponsors of this report, this is evidence against Dr. Jonathan?

Has it occurred to these demented persons that this is precisely what a genuine statesman should do in times like these? In September of 2011, in search of peace, former President Olusegun Obasanjo visited Maiduguri to see the family of the late founder of Boko Haram, Mohammed Yusuf. He was applauded for such a courageous act, as he should have been, because that is what is expected of statesmen.

In other climes, they give people Nobel Peace Prizes for prevailing on belligerents to sheathe their swords, but apparently in Nigeria, it is evidence of your complicity. Should Nigerians be surprised then that passers-by refuse to help those attacked by armed robbers or accident victims on the roadside like the Good Samaritan? If you do, the government may accuse you of being the perpetrator instead of the savior.

But these happenings are not surprising to me. We were all witnesses to the threat to withdraw the licenses of the two major fertilizer manufacturers in Nigeria, Notore Petrochemical and Indorama Eleme Petrochemical, for providing the materials used by terrorists and militants to make Improvised Explosive Devices (IEDs).

Now, according to this new tale inserted into the media, it was Dr. Jonathan who instructed militants to mine oil installations before the May 29th, 2015 handover date.

Now it is confirmed that liars do not have a good memory and so must contradict themselves. If the oil installations were rigged with mines the question to be asked is are mines made from fertilizers? Can they not get their story right?

There is a troubling pattern here. It seems that any time Dr. Jonathan is advancing on the world stage for his humanitarian and pro-democracy activities, these fallacious stories appear in the media to distract him.

When he was on his very successful international speaking tour earlier in the year, the lie was told that he was away on exile.

Now that he is back from his second successful outing as head of the African Union Election Observation Mission to Zambia, the usual suspects are up to their old tricks. Who knows what they would do next when they behold the great things that Dr. Jonathan is set to do very shortly?

And to the Minister of Information, Dr. Lai Mohammed, who was quoted in the said report as saying "these allegations have refused to go away and those making the allegations are not backing out", let me remind him that there are allegations against him that have refused to go away.

In fact, the allegations against Lai Mohammed come with documentary evidence. We remember that he was alleged to have begged his subordinates at the National Broadcasting Commission (NBC) for a 'loan' of ₦13 million against civil service rules and against the rules of public decency.

Have those allegations gone away, Mr. Lai Mohammed? Should we then accept them as true? Of course not! Why? Because allegations, no matter how weighty, are not evidence.

Like I said before, I am ever proud of Dr. Goodluck Jonathan. Somebody asked me what I gained by working with Goodluck Jonathan. My response was that I learnt wisdom. I learnt that It is better to lose power and gain honor than to gain power and lose honor. I learnt not to defend myself when my enemies falsely accuse me. The same media that gleefully reported their lies will eventually expose them when they see that the public is no longer buying their lies.

Finally, I learnt that the best revenge against those who criticize how you do your job is to step aside and let them have the job and watch them under perform in such a manner until they get so desperate that the only achievements they can boast of are the ones you achieved during your so-called under performance. May God bless Dr. Jonathan for teaching me such wisdom! In Jesus name.

Chapter 6
EDUCATION AND HUMILITY:
THE SECRET WEAPON BEHIND JONATHAN

Goodluck Jonathan was born on the 20th of November, 1957 in Otuoke, in the then Eastern Region of Nigeria to Lawrence Jonathan, a boat maker, and his wife Eunice Jonathan, a home maker.

It is necessary to cite his origin to show that Goodluck Jonathan was born without a silver spoon and without a big strong hand to push him through the vicissitudes of life. He has gotten to where he is today by the grace of God who blessed his hard work.

When Dr. Jonathan became President on May 6, 2010, many people were surprised at his passion for education which saw him giving education the highest sectoral allocation in the Federal budgets throughout his five-year term, all of which led to building fourteen new federal universities including twelve in states that had previously not had any such university. He also built 165 almajiri schools all over Northern Nigeria.

Dr. Jonathan did this because he was quite conversant that what leveled the playing field and helped him achieve things that were hitherto the exclusive preserve of children of the rich and powerful, was education.

In fact, from his early youth, Dr. Jonathan showed an aptitude for academics and made very good grades throughout his time as a student. In June of 1975, Dr. Goodluck Jonathan sat for his West African School Certificate Examinations and made the following results:

A2 economics

A2 biology

A2 chemistry

A2 Geography

A3 CRK

C6 English

C5 physics

A3 Literature in English*

Mathematics was canceled, so the next year he wrote the General Certificate of Education, GCE, in November and made 5 additional As including A3 in mathematics. So, before you call my Jonathan 'clueless', please show me your own champion's School Certificate result.

And by the way, Dr. Jonathan has his original certificates!

Moreover, in the year of our Lord, 1981, Dr. Goodluck Jonathan graduated with a Second Class Honours Upper Division degree in Zoology from the University of Port Harcourt, Rivers State. At that time, there was nothing like cash-for-grades in Nigeria. If you were not intelligent you could not graduate with such high scores.

And yet, a Senator who has been exposed to have a Third-Class degree and a former (?) dictator whose School Certificate status is yet to be determined had the temerity to once call such a man 'clueless'.

Dr. Jonathan may be a simple man who uses plain words and does not have any airs around himself, but that does not mean he is not an intellectual. He may not have been dictatorial and domineering while in office, but that did not make him any less effective as a leader.

In fact, the use of big grammar is not a sign of intelligence. It is like using too much make up to hide the fact that you are not beautiful. The more beautiful a woman is, the less make up she uses. The more intelligent a man, the simpler the language he uses.

Think of it like this: Jesus is the most intelligent man that ever lived, yet His language is so simple that the common people of Israel got Him. But satan is so foolish for rebelling against God, and He inspired the Pharisees, whose language was so complicated that the ordinary people did not understand them!

Many have mistaken this Christ-like quality of humility in Dr. Goodluck Jonathan and time and time again, events preceding their misjudgment keep proving to them how wrong they were.

Elsewhere in this book, I painstakingly listed the many achievements of Dr. Goodluck Jonathan and I do not need to restate them, but permit me to throw light on one or two incidents that show that the brain is greater than brawn.

On January 25, 2011 the Arab Spring began in Egypt. In less than a week after that date, then President Goodluck Jonathan issued an Executive Order for Nigerians to be evacuated from Egypt. On the 1st of February, 2011, Nigeria became the First Nation to evacuate her citizens out of Egypt. When the Arab Spring spread to Libya in February of 2011, President Jonathan ordered evacuations there which began on Thursday, February 24, 2011.

Also, when the Ebola Virus struck in Nigeria in 2014, the Goodluck Jonathan administration wasted no time in mobilizing against the disease alongside the affected state governments. Preventive measures were put in our airports and those affected were quarantined.

As a result of the decisiveness and the resolve of then President Jonathan, there was a unity of purpose in the country that transcended party, religion, region, ethnicity and economic status.

The end result was that Nigeria which had her first experience with the Ebola Virus on July 20, 2014, was declared Ebola Virus free on October 20, 2014, which made her the first nation to defeat Ebola and the fastest nation to do so after conquering the scourge in a mere three months.

Today, the Nigerian Defense Academy accepts female cadets after over half a century of operation. Also, thanks to Dr. Goodluck Jonathan who introduce an affirmative action that gave women a 35% slot of appointive positions at the federal level.

This goes to show that Jonathan was able to project Nigeria as a pacesetting nation by making quality decisions rather than by force of aggression.

This perhaps explains the statement made by US Congresswoman Sheila Jackson Lee (Democrat, Texas) at Congress on February 2, 2017 when she said, "I am inspired by Jonathan"!

And even his pattern of life shows that Dr. Jonathan is a stable person who has taken both pain and pleasure in his life with equanimity.

At age 59, he has only been a member of one political party all his life and does not own any account or property outside Nigeria. Such exemplary conduct is rare not just in Africa, but globally.

That is why I am personally pained when I read comments by those in power claiming that Dr. Goodluck Jonathan ruined Nigeria.

Perhaps Jonathan ruined Nigerian by reviving our previously moribund railways and making it possible for you to travel by rail from Lagos to Kano at a cost of.₦1500? Perhaps he ruined Nigeria by building the ONLY standard gauge modern railway that makes it possible for Nigerians to live in Kaduna and work in Abuja?

The fact remains that Nigeria thrived and became the third fastest growing economy in the world under Dr. Goodluck Jonathan because of two sterling qualities of the man who headed that administration.

Firstly, Jonathan is the most educated person ever to have become President of Nigeria.

And his enlightenment permeated his administration such that his cabinet had more PhDs and world class technocrats and professionals than any other in Nigeria's history.

In fact, after leaving his cabinet, many of his appointees have gone on to head several world and continental bodies including the World Bank and the African Development Bank.

And secondly, Jonathan has the humility to recognize that he is only a pencil in the hand of God. He is secure enough to acknowledge his weaknesses by surrounding himself with people who helped him compensate for them.

And these two qualities yielded positive results for Nigerians such that in 2010, Gallup polls rated Nigeria under Jonathan as the 'happiest nation on earth". In 2014, Nigeria under Jonathan had her best improvement in Transparency International's Corruption Perception Index, moving from 144 to 136. Incidentally, Nigeria has not made any improvements since then.

These sum up the fact that until a future administration comes along and tops these indices, history will be kind to Jonathan and the five years between 2010 to 2015 will be regarded as Nigeria's golden years.

Chapter 7
YOUWIN FROM THE EYES OF
AN OXFORD SCHOLAR

In September of 2016, President Jonathan gave a speech on youth empowerment at the University of Oxford Student Union. Before the event, he met with some students and faculty from the university who were engaged in research relevant to the presentation. One student who attended the meeting, a post-graduate researcher named James Burton, was partway through conducting a study into the Jonathan administration's YouWin program. The president was pleased to hear the initiative had engendered such academic interest and asked to see his findings. Though he and many other researchers continue to study the program, James agreed to summarize in this chapter, his current research into YouWin's effectiveness.

The problem of Nigeria's unemployed youth is well known. With 190 million people and a yearly population growth rate of almost 3%, Nigeria has by far the fastest growing population of the world's 10 most populous nations. The Nigerian economy needs to grow rapidly to maintain its population's current standard of living and find jobs for almost 2 million new job seekers a year.

Nigeria has a median age of 18.3 years old and its youth suffer the most from this lack of employment. The Nigerian National Bureau of Statistics puts the rate of youth under or unemployed at 45.66%. This not only has the obvious implications for the wellbeing of young people, but also hinders productivity and economic growth as well as contributing to crime, violence, unrest, and radicalization.

In this context, small entrepreneurial firms have emerged as an important economic contributor and vehicle for productively engaging Nigeria's youth. However, most entrepreneurs find it difficult to grow their firms to a size where they can to begin to employ others. World Bank survey data shows that in 2014, 99.6% of Nigerian firms had fewer than 10 workers and the modal firm size in most developing countries remains just one person, the owner.

The Jonathan government wanted to make measurable impact on this problem during their four-year term. They created the Youth Enterprise with Innovation in Nigeria (YouWin) program as a key part of this strategy. The program used the largest business plan competition ever created in Nigeria as a vehicle to support young people to start or grow their ventures such that they could employ others. It was administered by the Jonathan administration ministries of Finance, Communication Technology, and Youth Development with support from the World Bank and UK Department for International Development.

The competition was open to anyone between the ages of 18 and 40, with winners spread across the country's six regions and awards going to firms from an array of sectors. Before taking final submissions, the program offered a free business plan and writing course to over 6000 finalists to level the playing field for those who had not prepared such documents before.

The process to select the final winners was largely administered by independent organizations and was carefully built to maximize transparency and accountability. Business plans were anonymized then sent to be judged by a team from the Enterprise Development Centre in Lagos and consultants from Price Waterhouse Coopers, with further independent marking and quality control from UK based Plymouth Business School. Finally, winners were awarded a grant of between 1 and 10 million Naira, depending on the requirements and viability of the submitted proposals. Awardees also received further training and mentorship as they grew their businesses.

Over time, the program has been refined and improved, introducing an interview phase in the selection process, as well as more intensive training and closer monitoring. The first two rounds of the competition supported 1,200 each, while the third supported 1,500 entrepreneurs.

The Work Bank funded and conducted a comprehensive independent impact evaluation of the first round of the program, led by senior economist David McKenzie. After 3 years of panel data had been collected, the results were published in late 2015. The first round of YouWin gave 9.24 billion Naira in grants and cost around 319 million Naira to administer. The study found that the by the end of the program's third year it had directly generated approximately 7,027 jobs. Thus, the cost per job created was approximately 1.4 million Naira (8,538 USD) per job.

When compared with efforts specifically targeted at employment generation around the world, the numbers are deeply impressive. McKenzie found that YouWin was two and halftimes as efficient as a 2013 management consulting program in Mexico, four and a halftimes as efficient as a 2014 wage subsidy program in Jordan and almost ten times as efficient as a 2011 vocational training program in Turkey. YouWin even compared favourably with United States fiscal stimulus, proving 44% more efficient than government spending and 130% more efficient than tax cuts.

What's more, McKenzie made his comparisons based on the extremely conservative assumption that all YouWin firms would close-down the year his study concluded. In fact, YouWin surveys taken in October 2016 show that YouWin-1 awardees currently employ 7951 people, Youwin-2 awardees employ 6572 people and Youwin-3 awardees employ 11,816 people. Such figures need to be discounted somewhat because awardees tend to exaggerate their success when reporting to their benefactors. However, even the most conservative analysis shows that the program's results continue to become more impressive with every year the awardees stay in business. These YouWin numbers also do not consider the multiplier effects; the impact of new employees spending their wages, expansion of suppliers, increased tax revenues and overall productivity gains.

McKenzie also found several other impressive sets of results. 3 years after the competition, applicants who started new firms with their winnings were 37% more likely than non-winners to be operating a business and 23% more likely to have a firm with 10 or more workers. Winners with existing firms were 20% more likely to have survived and 21% more likely to employ 10+ workers. Awardees who started new businesses had 32% more sales and 23% more profits, while winners who applied with existing businesses enjoyed a 63% increase in sales and a 25% increase in profits. The program also made firms more innovative, with McKenzie noting that awardees introduced more new products, quality control systems, internal processes, pricing and sales channel than non-awardees.

McKenzie concluded that 'The YouWin business plan competition has had large impacts on the rate of business start-up, survival of existing firms, employment, profits, and sales of winning firms.' Other researchers have been less reserved in expressing their enthusiasm. Christopher Blattman, a Professor at the University of Chicago and associate of the United States Bureau of Economic Research, described YouWin as a contender for 'the most effective development program in history'.

My in-depth interviews with over 50 Nigerian entrepreneurs, half of which are YouWin awardees and half who applied for the program unsuccessfully, has suggested several clear reasons for the program's success in facilitating business growth.

Primarily, YouWin effectively gave awardees the resources to overcome key barriers to growing their businesses and helped them to mitigate the risks of operating an early stage venture in Nigeria's challenging business environment. It allowed tailors who were forced to use foot powered sewing machines when central power failed to buy generators and grow large enough to pay for the fuel. It provided the reputation and collateral for a cassava farmer to finance the construction of a full processing plant. It meant that transportation companies could buy better quality vehicles that required less maintenance. It provided a cushion in a volatile economy and the space to make the simple inevitable mistakes of a first-time entrepreneur. It gave local businesses the time to show the market that Nigerian made products can compete on the international stage, that a Nigerian cobbler with Nigerian leather can produce shoes to rival the quality of Italian imports.

For many, the grant meant moving operations from the living room to proper commercial premises, employing staff, investing in marketing for the first time, registering the enterprise and seeking regulatory approval. In short, it turned half-baked ideas, side projects and subsistence enterprises into fully functioning businesses.

This impact was particularly pronounced because micro and small businesses in Nigeria have little access to the kind of funds that offered such benefits as YouWin. Banks are slow and risk adverse, seldom lending without substantial collateral in the form of land and fixed assets. If loans are successful, the young businesses must take on the burden of servicing interest that can be as high as 30% annually.

The problem is compounded for ventures in more innovative and less traditional sectors. One awardee, the founder of a robotics company that went on to produce everything from hand held consumer devices to military grade drones, complained that financiers did not understand what a robotics company did in the early days and largely still don't. He applied to several banks before YouWin and despite showing clear market need and healthy financials, he was unsuccessful in every case. The founder of a recycling company tells a similar story. He approached all the major banks for loans before YouWin and was turned away. As it happened, his wife worked behind the desk of a microfinance institution at the time and he recalls how dejectedly he approached her with his hat in hand, only to be denied equally quickly. The equipment he purchased with his YouWin grant helped him to grow the business from an annual turnover of around 500,000 Naira to 50 million Naira in just under 2 years.

YouWin supported many entrepreneurs that were not independently wealthy and could not have simply borrowed necessary capital from friends and family. Without such financing, most respondents felt that their firms would be years behind in growth or have been forced to close their doors by now. Though many of them overestimate this impact, the McKenzie data shows that plenty of them are right.

Beyond financial support, the president also took a special interest in the YouWin awardees, many see him as the father of their businesses and display pictures of or with him in their offices. In 2014, Jonathan called for an exhibition in Abuja which allowed many of the successful awardees to model their products. He went around to each stall individually, meeting the entrepreneurs and admiring what they had produced.

After the event, he asked for sit down meetings with a sample of the awardees. One such entrepreneur remembers the experience vividly. He describes Jonathan's protocol staff prepping the awardees on what to say and what not to say to the president. They were to be entirely complementary about their experience. However, as the young business owner tells it, the president immediately threw protocol out the window, dismissing his staff and requesting one-on-one meetings with each participant.

The president asked them what barriers they faced and how he could help. In this case, the entrepreneur explained that he had been having great trouble getting approval for his products from the National Agency of Food and Drug Administration and Control (NAFDAC). He complained that small businesses could not afford to jump through endless hoops, wait months for feedback or pay consultants to help them navigate the process. Within weeks, the president had mandated that there be an expedited NAFDAC process for Small and Medium enterprise and a specific desk was set up to service their needs. Some YouWin awardees even had their application fees waived entirely.

Finally, it is important to acknowledge that such support, like loans, consultants, tax cuts and training, is only as effective as the entrepreneurs themselves. YouWin was uniquely powerful at picking winners but it did not run any of the businesses. Ultimately, it was the ingenuity, daring and perseverance of Nigerian entrepreneurs that created jobs. The Global Entrepreneurship Monitor finds that Nigeria has one of the largest proportions of aspiring entrepreneurs in the world and much more needs to be done to support them. While YouWin was a highly efficient program, its scope was far too small to have a significant impact on unemployment rates in Nigeria.

To have a large-scale impact, policy makers must both pursue broad structural economic change that increases productivity and competitiveness, as well as allocate more resources to targeted programs such as YouWin. To do so may not be politically easy. When the Jonathan government first proposed YouWin, it was heavily criticized and many still doubt its efficacy despite clear evidence in its favour. Giving such large sums to so many early stage firms in a country like Nigeria was unheard of five years ago and, though the World Bank and many other organizations are now looking to replicate YouWin's success, the model remains rare. Hopefully, future African heads of state will see similar potential in their own entrepreneurs and have the courage to support it.

Chapter 8
EL-RUFAI VINDICATES JONATHAN AND INDICTS BUHARI

Recently I had cause to read the memorandum to President Muhammadu Buhari by his mini me, Malam Nasir El-Rufai, the Governor of Kaduna state. All I can say is, wow!

I guess President Muhammadu Buhari now believes his former boss, ex President Olusegun Obasanjo, who wrote of Malam Nasir El-Rufai in his book, My Watch Volume 11 thus:

'I recognised his weaknesses; the worst being his inability to be loyal to anybody or any issue consistently for long, but only to Nasir el-Rufai.'

If only Professor John Paden had been patient enough to wait for the release of ElRufai's memorandum to President Muhammadu Buhari, he would not have so effusively praised the President. Having done so through his book 'Muhammadu Buhari-The Challenges of Leadership in Nigeria', Paden now comes across as a revisionist at best and a liar at worst because we now have a situation where even die hard loyalists of the Buhari administration have come to accept the reality that Nigeria is faring much worse under the status quo than it did under the previous Peoples Democratic Party administration of Dr. Goodluck Jonathan.

President Muhammadu Buhari and the All Progressive Congress called Dr. Goodluck Jonathan 'clueless' and promised change but look at the change they brought! The same Nasir El-Rufai that called Jonathan clueless now calls Muhammadu Buhari's administration clueless without having used that particular word.

The Buhari led APC administration overturned much of the good initiatives of the Jonathan era. The former President gave us YouWIN but this administration stopped it and today YOU LOSE as a Nigerian youth. Dr. Goodluck Jonathan brought the Presidential Special Scholarship Scheme for Innovations and Development to train First Class graduates abroad, this government stopped it so Nigerian youths cannot benefit yet children of the APC elite almost exclusively school abroad.

They fought Jonathan and the PDP tooth and nail over subsidy, calling it a scam, today the same APC has increased petrol price and subsidy still remains. They said ₦199 to $1 under Jonathan was "unacceptable", but ₦500 to $1 under President Buhari is acceptable. They said the Jonathan administration did not build infrastructure, yet President Buhari commissioned Abuja-Kaduna railway built and completed by the previous government. Can you now see that we are dealing with "desperate power-seekers with empty promises" as Jonathan himself warned us on December 11, 2014?

In 2010, Gallup polls rated Nigeria under Goodluck Jonathan as the 'happiest nation on earth". In 2017 under President Muhammadu Buhari we are not even the happiest nation in Africa. We are rated 6th happiest in Africa! In 2014, Nigeria under Jonathan had her best improvement in Transparency International's Corruption Perception Index, moving from 144 to 136. We have not made any improvements under the so called anti-corruption administration of President Muhammadu Buhari.

You can fool gullible Nigerians, but you cannot fool the world. Jonathan fired any of his ministers involved in conflict of interest not to talk of corruption, including Professor Barth Nnaji and Stella Oduah. President Buhari on the other hand prefers to write letters defending his own Secretary to the Government of the Federation, a man caught RED HANDED in the grass cutting contract corruption. And they want us to be deceived that there is an anti corruption war in Nigeria. I am sorry for any one who still believes in that fairytale!

That Nigerians believed the APC's lies proves we are more malleable than an amoeba. A woman who believes every man ends up with empty promises and unwanted pregnancies. To those who believed/believe the APC, I have some questions for you: Where is your $1 to ₦1? Where is your ₦40 per liter petrol? Where is your job seekers allowance? Where is your uninterrupted power? Where is the promise to lead from the front? Where is the 740,000 "immediate relief jobs for graduates"? Where is the three million jobs in three years? But the real question though is where is your brain if you actually believed these promises?

And if you are still deceived, I will urge you to undeceive yourself by reading El-Rufai's memorandum. It is being sold by vendors on the street and I love the shortened title they have given it.

Whereas El-Rufai gave the memorandum the highfalutin title of 'IMMEDIATE AND MEDIUM TERM IMPERATIVES FOR PRESIDENT MUHAMMADU BUHARI', these young vendors gave it its real title 'El-Rufai to Buhari: You Have Failed'! Chikena! No long turenci!

In a combination of punches which the President may find hard to survive, El-Rufai said, and I quote:

"In very blunt terms, Mr. President, our APC administration has not only failed to manage expectations of a populace that expected overnight 'change' but has failed to deliver even mundane matters ofgovernance"

Oh Mr. President, what a pity, what a pity! First your own wife warns you that she may not even campaign for you in 2019, then your political khalifa, the magajin Buhari in the person of Nasir El-Rufai, calls you a failure! If you consigned your wife to the 'other room' as punishment, to which room will you consign El-Rufai? Let me recommend a room for you. How about the kitchen? I am sure you have some knives there. El-Rufai will find them handy in practicing his favorite hobby-backstabbing.

Yes, I agree with Nasir El-Rufai that Buhari has failed, but then Nasir El-Rufai lacks the moral authority to say that because one, he is one of those that promoted Buhari to Nigerians and two, he has also failed in Kaduna state.

What notable thing has he achieved in Kaduna? Just as Buhari has taken Nigeria backward, Nasir El-Rufai has also taken Kaduna backward.

There was relative peace in Kaduna before El-Rufai became Governor, but is there peace today? Absolutely not. Because of his careless comments and even more careless actions, the security situation has so deteriorated in Kaduna that more people are dying in Kaduna from Fulani herdsmen than in Borno from Boko Haram.

In 2012, El-Rufai wrote an article on the back page of This Day and stated that Anambra state was one of the poorest states in Nigeria.

Today, in the year 2016, Anambra state is one of the richest states in Nigeria and for the past four years they have topped the list of states with the best WAEC results. Anambra does not owe workers and rejected the Federal Government's bail out. Anambra does not borrow. Anambra exports vegetables to Europe and grows its own rice.

In contrast, under El-Rufai as Governor of Kaduna, Kaduna state in 2017 is by far poorer than Anambra state that el-Rufai said was one of Nigeria's poorest states in 2012.

Kaduna owes workers salary, Kaduna is heavily indebted and had to be bailed out by the federal government. The state economy has deteriorated badly.

Yet their governor, el-Rufai was laughing at Anambra in 2012. Today

Anambra state is laughing at him.

And to those who consider themselves to be amongst the privileged class of 97 percenters, the speedy and one sided arrest of the perpetrators of the Ife Hausa/Yoruba clash of March 2017 shows that even if you think you are among the 97%, if it is not Panadol it cannot be the same as Panadol! A slave that laughs when his fellow slave is buried in a shallow grave obviously does not know that the same fate awaits him on death.

Let us consider the following trend very carefully: Shiite massacre-no arrest. Southern Kaduna killings-little or no arrest. Agatu genocide-little or no arrest. Pastor Eunice Elisha murdered in broad daylight in Kubwa-No arrest. Evangelist Bridget Agbahime beheaded in broad daylight in Kano-suspected killers discharged and acquitted on the instruction of the state Attorney General. Ife clashes-Plenty of lopsided arrests. Is this how justice works in the new and improved Nigeria under President Muhammadu Buhari?

Why is the Ife crisis so special that a government that arrested no one when hundreds of Shiites were slaughtered has sudden gone on an arresting spree? Are some lives more important than others in today's Nigeria? Is it that the only time this government acts speedily is when cows and the cream of the 97% are affected?

In March of 2017, the Abuja office of global human rights watch dog, Amnesty International, was attacked by hoodlums.

This came shortly after they had released a very negative report on the state of human rights under the Buhari administration. Amnesty International also released a damming report during the PDP administration of President Jonathan but nobody invaded their offices! Instead that government released its own intelligently written rebuttal to Amnesty International's report and the independent observer could compare the two and come to an informed conclusion.

You do not need to defend the truth. You only need to unleash it and it will defend itself!

When you bring in protesters to protest the truth, discerning people think of those timeless words of Queen Gertrude in Shakespeare's Hamlet "The lady doth protest too much, methinks"!

And it is certain that the Amnesty International protesters protested too much as it has come to be revealed through pictures that can not lie, that they were paid. If you have not seen the pictures then you need to Google them.

So sad that under a so called anti corruption administration, jobless people were hired to protest against Amnesty International. Are we now seeing the modus operandi that the Buhari administration will use to fulfill its campaign promises of providing 740,000 immediate relief jobs and 3,000,000 jobs in three years? Since the President returned from his 'vacation', there have been many pro-Buhari rallies. They accused the PDP of providing jobs for the boys meanwhile they provide jobs for protesters. Now we know the secret. Very sad!!

This episode is not the only event that puts the hypocrisy of this administration on display. Imagine my surprise to have read the headline on the Punch Newspapers on Wednesday the 22nd of March. The headline went thus 'Buhari condemns fake certificates, exam fraud'! Oh the irony! The sheer audacious irony of that headline!

It took mere hours for President Muhammadu Buhari to condemn the U.K. terror attack, but it took him months to comment on (not condemn, he merely commented) on the Southern Kaduna killings. When the President was 'resting' in London, it was Nigerians, not English people that were holding prayer vigils for him. Four people died in the U.K. Hundreds have died in Southern Kaduna.

Chapter 9
THE MANY LIES IN JOHN PADEN'S BOOK ON BUHARI

The book 'Muhammadu Buhari-The Challenges of Leadership in Nigeria' by Professor John Paden is not only an intellectually lazy work, it is also a fallacious document hastily put together to paint the protagonist in the borrowed garb of an effective leader who is cleaning the Augean Stable of misrule and corruption in Nigeria, but my question is this-how can you fight corruption with lies?

I have taken my time to x-ray the book and I cannot help but agree with the national leader of the ruling All Progressive Congress that Paden has done a great disservice to the truth. If I were Paden, I would consider a career in fiction writing. His talents are much better suited for that than to scholarly and investigative work.

On page 52 of the book, Professor Paden declares that Dr. Goodluck Jonathan declared for the April 2011 Presidential election on Saturday, 18th of September 2011.

But for a man who was a Rhodes scholar at Oxford University, Paden did not show much scholarliness because if he did, he would have established that Dr. Jonathan made world history by being the first ever Presidential candidate to make his declaration on the social media platform, facebook, on Wednesday the 15th of September, 2016, a feat which was featured on the New York Times, the Washington Post and in several international news media.

If this was the only error in the book, one could forgive Paden, but the errors go on and on.

For example on page 53, Paden, without citing any proof or evidence, called Dr. Jonathan's margin of victory in the South south and Southeast 'nonsensical', but then he goes ahead to accept President Buhari's margin of victory in the North as valid even though they mirrored Dr. Jonathan's margins in the South.

On page 55, Paden called to question Jonathan's handling of the economy but then in page 60 he admits that the 7% GNP growth Nigeria attained under Jonathan was "impressive". Does Paden suffer from a split personality? Here he is calling into question former President Jonathan's ability to manage an economy that he himself admits generated an impressive growth yet he is praising a President Buhari under whom Nigeria has gone into recession. I don't get it Paden!

Perhaps Paden should have written a book singing Jonathan's praises instead of President Buhari's!

Then he attacks Dr. Jonathan in page 55 over the 2012 attempt to remove fuel subsidies and pointed to the street protests that broke out in reaction, but curiously failed to mention that such protests were instigated and led by the then opposition members including President Buhari's former running mate, Pastor Tunde Bakare, who was openly at the fore front of the protests and Malam Nasir Elrufai, who coordinated activities during the Occupy Nigeria protests. This is nothing short of intellectual dishonesty.

In page 59, Paden says 'President Jonathan had signed a pledge in 2011 to run for only one term'. This is just a lie and betrays the fact that Professor Paden might have replaced investigation with gossip as a means of gathering information. I make bold to say that if Professor Paden can produce a copy of the signed pledge then I would give him a million dollars!

On page 65, Paden goes ad hominem saying "President Jonathan seemed more focused on hanging onto power by looting the public treasury".

The above is nothing short of libel. But before he is made to answer for his lies in court, let me ask Paden a simple question. If what he wrote about Dr. Jonathan looting the treasury is true, then how come Nigeria was able to have what he himself agrees was an 'impressive' economic growth and how come Nigeria made progress on the annual Transparency International Corruption Perception Index?

On page 67, showing his inability to give credit to whom it is due, Paden accused Jonathan of appointing partisan and dishonest Resident Electoral Commissioners for States so they could assist the People's Democratic Party (PDP) rig elections but praised INEC Chairman Professor Attahiru Jega for his honesty. What he failed to mention is that it was President Jonathan who nominated and appointed the honest Jega without having ever met him and that it is this same honest Jega that was fully in charge of posting officials to states to serve as Resident Electoral Commissioners and who (along with his board) had power to recall and discipline any REC.

Then in page 68, Paden outdid himself as a liar when he said "faced with these results, would Jonathan concede, or would he challenge the results in court?"

Paden continues on his lying spree by saying inter alia that 'several former African heads of state held private meetings with Jonathan....they insisted... that he accept the results". Not yet done with his fallacies, Paden continues "there was considerable international pressure on Jonathan, including by the Archbishop of Canterbury and Western Diplomats".

All these are the figment of the imagination of either Paden or his sources.

To prove that Paden is a liar, I will quote Mansur Liman, the editor of the BBC Hausa Service in Nigeria, who was at the INEC Elections Result Center in Abuja WHILE results were being released.

Mr. Liman testified verbally on the BBC Hausa service and in writing on its website that while results were still being AWAITED and BEFORE INEC had declared Buhari as winner of the election, he had placed a call to the Buhari campaign and testified that his contact within the Buhari campaign "told me that Gen Buhari had just received a phone call from his rival, in which the president conceded and congratulated him."

Testifying further, Mr. Liman said that the report he received indicated that "the president (President Jonathan) took the decision to make the call without consulting anyone. They told me that if he had talked to some of his advisers, they would have objected."

This is a direct testimony from a man on the ground with timelines and records that can stand up in court. Are we to jettison his eyewitness and substantial documentary evidence for the unsubstantiated lies of Paden?

But even without taking into account Liman's testimony, I traveled to London after making calls to one of the Archbishop of Canterbury's closest and most senior aides and after a face to face interview with one of the people involved I have established beyond reasonable doubt that the Archbishop of Canterbury DID NOT call Dr. Jonathan to mount pressure on him to concede.

Paden lied!!

This is a direct quote from an official in the Palace of Lambeth when I interviewed him on Paden's claims-"that is nonsense. The Archbishop did not call to put pressure on President Jonathan to concede. He called AFTER President Jonathan had conceded to congratulate him for conceding!"

I urge Nigerian newspapers to reach out to the Palace of Lambeth to investigate John Paden's claims themselves. Both Paden and his source are liars!

If anybody has a history of problems conceding when he was defeated, that person is none other than President Muhammadu Buhari himself. In his three previous unsuccessful attempts at the Presidency, not once did Muhammadu Buhari ever concede much less congratulate the victor. Instead, his comments when he lost were at best uncharitable and at worst unpatriotic!

But oh, there are more lies in Paden's book.

In page 195, Paden lies again when he said that in May of 2016 while Dr. Jonathan was in the US, he had to "cancel some of his public engagements because of protests by Nigerians living abroad".

This lie is so easy to disprove. Dr. Jonathan did not cancel any events. He could not attend two events in California and he asked me to represent there. The two events were his Keynote speech at the California State University in Sacramento and his leadership award by two California cities.

The truth of the matter is that Dr. Jonathan took ill and it was the officials of Nigeria's mission in New York who actually took him to hospital. Both Dr. Paden and President Buhari can call the head of Mission in New York to confirm if this is true.

And lies are not the main problem of Paden's book. The main problem is that for a book on President Buhari, Paden's book places too much focus on blaming others for the President's shortcomings.

One would have thought that such a book would at least talk of President Buhari's achievements, but on second thought, when you have a President who has little or no achievements, I suppose you would have to make do with lies and accusations as fillers for a book on him otherwise such a book would be very slim.

Let me end by saying that no matter how close Professor Paden thinks he is to President Buhari, he cannot be as close to him as the President's own wife and mother of his kids.

After he finished giving his procured and false whitewashed verdict of the President, the President's wife gave the real verdict on President Buhari just a week ago as follows: "if things continue like this up to 2019, I will not go out and campaign again and ask any woman to vote like I did before. I will never do it again."

No wonder that while Paden devotes over 60 pages of his 284 page book to former President Jonathan, he only devotes a few sentences in two pages (36-37) to the President's wife, Aisha Buhari. Of course, he tried unsuccessfully not to call too much attention to the one person who could disprove all the lies in his book. Thank God for the courage of Aisha Buhari.

Chapter 10
JONATHAN'S PROPHECY, BUHARI'S HERESY AND TUFACE'S BRAVERY

On December 11, 2014, then President Goodluck Jonathan accepted the Presidential nomination of the Peoples Democratic Party to contest the 2015 Presidential elections as its candidate. At that occasion, the former leader made a statement which, in hindsight, can now be seen as a prophecy.

On that day, Jonathan said:

"The choice before Nigerians in the coming election is simple: A choice between going forward or going backwards; between the new ways and the old ways; between freedom and repression; between a record of visible achievements and beneficial reforms - and desperate power-seekers with empty promises."

When the Naira crashed to ₦500 to $1 on Monday the 30th of January, 2017 it hit me that Dr. Jonathan's prophecy had been fulfilled.

I remember (and I am sure you can too) the giant billboards the APC erected all over the country saying, and I quote

'Is ₦216 to $1 okay? It is time to act now. Buhari-Osinbajo'.

Well both President Muhammadu Buhari and Vice President Yemi Osinbajo have 'acted' for almost two years now and today it is now over ₦500 to $1. It is time for the duo to answer their own question.

On the 20th of November, 2014, a certain young Nigerian named Mohammad had tweeted the following tweet on Twitter;

"Today a dollar N180 and a pound is N280, hope you have a family....this is really the transformation agenda..!! GEJ has finished Nigeria.."

This tweet went viral because the APC, through its agents on Twitter, retweeted the tweet until it trended online.

Flash forward to Monday the 30th of January, 2017, the day the Naira crossed over the ₦500 to $1 rubicon and the now sober Mohammad tweeted three times and I will quote each of those tweets on the next page:

The first tweet

"GEJ should please forgive me!!!"

The second tweet

"N500 even wen they claim the are fighting corruption #bringbackourGEJ"

The third tweet

"GEJ a true definition of the word HERO ...!!!"

This time around, though the APC refused to retweet Mohammad who tweets from the handle @deee009, his last tweets are even more popular than the first because Nigerians retweeted them, storyfied them and blogs celebrated them.

On Tuesday 31st of January, 2017, another young Nigerian named Uchenna tweeted through his twitter handle, Uchez2 this:

"@Uchez2: How did the dollar stay at ₦175-₦200 for 4yrs under "massive looting"?

How is it now at N510 in 2 years under "massive savings"?"

What Jonathan's 2014 quote and Mohammad's 2014 and 2017 tweets as well as Uchenna's question has shown is that, no matter how far and fast falsehood has travelled, it must eventually be overtaken by truth.

Everybody is affected by the failed promises of the Buhari administration. The richest African and Black man in the world, Aliko Dangote, has seen his fortune depreciate by more than 50% from $25 billion under former President Jonathan to $12.4 billion today. We pray it does not shrink to $1.2 billion before 2019! There is no Nigerian that is not affected and that is all the more reason why the multiple award winning singer and rapper, Innocent Idibia, AKA Tuface has said he is going to lead a nationwide protest against the policies of this government which are impoverishing Nigerians. Of course very predictably, the administration, either directly or indirectly, has come out guns blazing against the much loved entertainer.

Government surrogates and jealous rivals have sought to disqualify and disenfranchise him from leading his protest by saying that as a father of seven children from three different mothers Tuface lacks the moral authority to protest against government policies!

First of all, the problem many of his celebrity haters have with Tuface is not the protest itself perse. They are really angry that they were not the ones who thought of it!

If having children from many women is their grouse then they would have had a grouse with many Nigerian leaders. Which Nigerian leader has children from only one woman? And it almost became comical when the Presidency asked to debate with Tuface on live TV. Really? A President who refused to debate his opponents at the Presidential Debates during the elections now wants Tuface to debate live on TV. I mean just negodu!

When some musicians and actors gathered at Ojota with Nasir Elrufai and Dino Melaye against then President Jonathan in February 2012, nobody cared how many children they had but suddenly they care about Tuface's baby mamas!

I guess both Elrufai and Dino Melaye have all their children from one woman!

In the new and improved Federal Republic of Double Standards, if you have more than one baby mama you can be a President, a Governor or a Senator, but you cannot lead a protest! It is haram! You are not morally fit to protest!

And it was so disappointing to see an official All Progressive Congres Twitter handle mocking the protest. APC News TV tweeted and I am quoting:

"@APCNEWSTV: JUST BEFORE YOU JOIN THE SENSELESS PROTEST, NOTE THAT! Godswill Akpabio bankrolled the posh wedding of 2face"

What rubbish! First of all, this is a desperate lie. But even if this were true (it is not) didn't Nigerians vote for President Muhammadu Buhari despite the fact that former Governors Rotimi Amaechi and Bola Tinubu bankrolled him?

If the Presidency and the APC want us to believe that Tuface Idibia's planned protest is "senseless" because his wedding was bankrolled by former Governor Godswill Akpabio then they are inadvertently admitting that President Buhari's Government is "senseless" because its election was bankrolled by Amaechi and Tinubu. That will explain a lot! It will explain the Presidency's senselessness in the matter regarding Supreme Court Justice Walter Onnoghen who has been denied what should have been his privilege by political tradition as well as by judicial precedent.

Ibrahim Magu is accused of corruption yet President Muhammadu Buhari insists on confirming him. Justice Walter Onnoghen is free from corruption yet President Buhari refuses to confirm him! This from a so called anti-corruption President. Is it because Magi is a Muslim from the North, while the other is a Christian from the South. This is yet another example in the series of double standards that are the hallmark of this administration.

A Government that publicly urged accused justices to immediately step down, yet writes copious and even verbose letters to justify why the provenly corrupt Secretary to the Government of the Federation, Babachir Lawal, continues to retain his post. In Nigeria, it seems there is one law for the 97 percenters and another for the 5 percenters. Again I say, welcome to President Buhari's new and improved Federal Republic of Double Standards!

What President Buhari is doing to Justice Walter Onnoghen is nothing short of judicial heresy. He is placing his parochial bias above a well established doctrine that seniority at the bar and bench is the major requirement for upward mobility in the legal profession. And as an aside, I am noticing that the rapidly shrinking army of the cult of Buhari are also set against the new U.S. President, Donald J Trump. And it got me thinking. I have a hunch that the problem Buharists have with Donald Trump are not his policies but the fact that a politician is actually doing what he promised to do during his campaign. They are so used to President Buhari, who promises one thing and does another thing, that when they finally see a leader who says what he will do and does what he says they go into shock.

In his first day in office, President Trump has already started fulfilling his promises. He has not blamed Obama, he has not blamed the state of things he met on the ground. He has rather began his tenure by focusing on his promises rather than focusing on the alleged wrongdoings of his predecessors. This is why many people who supported Nigerian President Buhari cannot stand Trump. Because he exposes the hypocrisy of someone who promised change and is delivering more of the same.

This is why they are so heavily invested in blame gaming the system and blaming every negative occurrence on previous administrations while waiting to give President Buhari credit for the few things that have gone right under his government which are, ironically, the handiwork of the very administrations that he denigrates.

Two days ago (January 31st of 2017) the Nigerian Bureau of Statistics revealed that foreign investments into Nigeria has dropped to a 10 year low. I am waiting to see the creativity with which the Buhari administration will come up with reasons to blame Goodluck Jonathan for this! Perhaps

Jonathan went around to all the nations of the world to convince them not to invest in Nigeria!

I thought that the Buhari government said Nigeria was a pariah state under Jonathan. How could a pariah government attract more investment than an acceptable government like the Buhari administration. You see, like I said previously in this piece, no matter how far and fast a lie has travelled, it MUST eventually be overtaken by truth. And it is silly of the Lagos State Police Command to say they would stop Tuface's protest! This is the sort of impunity that has become the norm under President Muhammadu Buhari. Doesn't Tuface have the Constitutional right of freedom of assembly? Does he not have the right to free speech?

The same security forces that cannot bring the killers of pastor Eunice Elisha to book, or give justice to the be-headers of Evangelist Bridget Agbahime have now found their voice when it comes to stopping the harmless Tuface. Is it not silly that at a time when the Directorate of State Security have not been able to utilize its man power to make any discernible impact in the war against terror they have the men to storm Apostle Johnson Suleiman's hotel room in Ado Ekiti?

At a time when we have a Governor confessing that he paid money to killers of the citizens he is constitutionally sworn to protect, at a time when Nigeria has overnight become the most dangerous place in the world to be a Christian, at a time when the dollar goes for ₦500 to $1, is it really Apostle Suleiman that is the problem of Nigeria? The Presidency called Apostle Suleiman's speech hate speech! Puh-leeze! What hate speech can be worse than President Buhari's 97% versus 5%? That a Presidency headed by a man who threatened that the "dog and baboon will all be soaked in blood" has the guts to ask the Christian Association of Nigeria to condemn Apostle Suleiman is the joke of the year. If the Presidency are looking for someone to condemn let them go to London!

Finally, let me say that the Father did not give Jesus a Name that is above all names because Jesus is intelligent. No. Lucifer is also intelligent. God promoted Jesus because of two qualities. Loyalty and Humility. When people ask me why I am loyal to former President Jonathan, they do not realize that I do not live my life for anybody whether it is Dr. Goodluck Jonathan or President Muhammadu Buhari or even Donald J. Trump. My life is a test and upon my death the Father will mark my test paper. I am loyal to ex-President Jonathan just as I try to be loyal to all my friends whether high or low because a disloyal and proud person is like Lucifer who tried to take The Father's Throne and a loyal person is like Jesus who had the opportunity to do the same yet chose to remain Loyal and Humble.

If I do not follow the Messiah's example, then my Christianity is questionable!

TO WHOM IT MAY CONCERN

STATEMENT OF RESULT

The Council has been requested by **Jonathan Goodluck Ebele E.** to furnish him with the details of his performance in the:

DECEMBER 1976 GCE O/L

The request was informed by a reported fire incident that gutted his residence.

Our records show that **Jonathan Goodluck Ebele E.** sat the examination at Port-Harcourt with Index Number **21716/165.** Details of his performance are as follows:

SUBJECT	GRADE
Geography	3(C)
Economics	1(A)
Mathematics	3(C)
Chemistry	3(C)
Biology	3(C)

SUBJECTS RECORDED FIVE (5)

Please, accord this Statement of Result the recognition it deserves.

Yours Faithfully,

CHIEF O. O. ADULOJU
SENIOR DEPUTY REGISTRAR/TA
cko

DR. IYI UWADIAE
HEAD OF NATIONAL OFFICE

West African Examinations Council

School Certificate

JUNE 1975

This is to Certify that: JONATHAN GOODLUCK EBELE

having been in attendance at the following recognised school

MATER DEI HIGH SCHOOL, IMIRINGI

sat the Joint Examination for the School Certificate and General Certificate of Education and qualified for the award of a School Certificate.

The Candidate obtained the following results

SUBJECT	GRADE	SCHOOL CERTIFICATE RESULT	GCE ORDINARY LEVEL EQUIVALENT
ENGLISH LANGUAGE	6	CREDIT	CREDIT
LITERATURE IN ENGLISH	4	CREDIT	CREDIT
BIBLE KNOWLEDGE	3	GOOD	GOOD
GEOGRAPHY	2	VERY GOOD	VERY GOOD
ECONOMICS	2	VERY GOOD	VERY GOOD
PHYSICS	5	CREDIT	CREDIT
CHEMISTRY	2	VERY GOOD	VERY GOOD
BIOLOGY	2	VERY GOOD	VERY GOOD
SUBJECTS RECORDED	EIGHT		

CD 82

CANDIDATE No. 2541065

Chairman of Council

CERTIFICATE No. SC 249030

Registrar to the Council

Any alteration or erasure renders this certificate valueless.

FEDERAL MINISTRY OF EDUCATION
OFFICE OF THE HONOURABLE MINISTER OF STATE
1st Floor, Federal Secretariat Complex, Phase 3, Shehu Shagari Way, Garki Abuja.
Telephone: 09-6280922, Website: www.fmegovng.org

Ref: HMSE/FME/147/VOL.1/150

12th March, 2014

His Excellency
Dr. Kashim Shettima
Executive Governor of Borno State
Maiduguri
Borno State

SECURITY CHALLENGES AND THE CONDUCT OF THE 2014 WASSCE, SSCE IN BORNO, YOBE AND PARTS OF ADAMAWA STATE

In view of the current security challenges in the North-East States of the Country, the West African Examinations Council (WAEC) and the National Examination Council of Nigeria (NECO) have expressed concerns over the safety of their Officers who will be deployed to supervise the conduct of the 2014 diet of the examination in your State.

2. In response to the concerns, I have directed that the candidates in the Federal Unity Schools be assembled in the respective state capital where they are to sit for the examination in safe locations. You are please enjoined to make contingency arrangements for candidates from public and private schools in your state to sit the examination in safe locations.

3. Details of your arrangements should be forwarded to the Federal Ministry of Education and the two examination bodies for their information and necessary action.

4. Please accept the assurances of my warmest regards.

BARR. EZENWO NYESOM WIKE
Supervising Minister of Education

INDEX

CPSIA information can be obtained
at www.ICGtesting.com
Printed in the USA
LVOW03s1457110617
537725LV00033B/1225/P